THE MANY FACES OF KATNISS EVERDEEN

Exploring the Heroine of The Hunger Games

VALERIE ESTELLE FRANKEL

The Many Faces of Katniss Everdeen

Exploring the Heroine of *The Hunger Games*

Zossima Press
a division of Winged Lion Press
Hamden, CT

CREDITS

"Katniss the Reality TV Star: Reflection in a Plastic Mirror" Reprinted from *Of Bread, Blood and THE HUNGER GAMES: Critical Essays on the Suzanne Collins Trilogy* © 2012 Edited by Mary F. Pharr and Leisa A. Clark. Series Editors Donald E. Palumbo and C.W. Sullivan III by permission of McFarland & Company, Inc., Box 611, Jefferson NC 28640. www.mcfarlandpub.com.

"What Young Adult Fantasies Reveal: *THE HUNGER GAMES*, *TWILIGHT*, and the Modern Heroine's Journey" National Women's Studies Conference, Oakland, CA, Nov 8-11, 2012. Unpublished conference proceedings.

Zossima Press

ISBN-13 978-1-936294-22-0

Table of Contents

INTRODUCTION

Like *Harry Potter* and *Twilight* before it, *The Hunger Games* has become a phenomenon. It boasted the third-largest opening weekend in movie history, the largest ever to star a female lead (also the largest that wasn't a sequel, since *Harry Potter and the Deathly Hallows, Part 2* and *The Dark Knight* were the others). Teachers are discussing the book in all levels of school. Blogs and articles crowd the internet. Etsy's bursting with cellphone covers, mockingjay lightbulbs, shirts, and jewelry. Even archery lessons are up. But most of all, teens and kids are devouring the books.

The series is getting kids reading, the same praise that *Harry Potter* earned. Like *Harry Potter*, the books offer something for everyone, from action-packed escapism to a far-off world with close, relatable characters. It's a survival action-adventure set in a creepy future with coming-of-age and romance thrown in the mix. There's a heroine's journey, a love triangle, a quest into the darkness of the soul. And unlike *Harry Potter*, the series stars a powerful olive-skinned girl who can outrun deer, keep her family alive, and outwit the highest levels of government. At last, a heroine who's far more than a love interest or sidekick has taken over pop culture.

David Levithan, editorial director at Scholastic, told the story of the book's first appearance at his company, noting, "We knew it was a crossover success because we were not only giving it to our kids, but we were also giving it to our parents and getting great responses from both, which was really the first inkling we had that it was gonna be huge for both teenagers and adults" ("Gamemaker").

The Hunger Games, at the time of this writing, has three more movies remaining. The first fan-based conference, Victory Tour 2013, is coming this summer. But there has already been an enormous body of scholarly and fannish work, in books, at pop culture and young adult literary conventions, and even at conventions for the competing franchises.

The term "competing" may be rather strong of course. 2012 marks the final *Twilight* movie, with the final *Harry Potter* a few years before. Both have mirrored *Hunger Games* in both the audience and the transmedia nature of the franchise: Fansites are exploding with art and fanfiction, with parody videos and cross-genre projects like "The Potter Games." *Saturday Night Live* and *Mad Magazine* have tackled it, tribute Halloween costumes and mockingjay pins are everywhere. Video games have been popular, though criticized for the violent recreations of the arena. A quieter family-friendly boardgame reproduces the pre-Game training.

In fact, many parents are critical of violence in the series, so much so that it's #3 in the ALA's top ten banned books for 2012, above *To Kill a Mockingbird* as #10. (Other reasons for its banned status include the inaccurate to the point of puzzling "sexually explicit" and "satanic/occult." In fact, there is no magic, witchcraft, devil worship or mention of these, and no romantic moments beyond kissing.) The series is violent, no question. However, many of those most offended haven't read the series to understand it's a *protest* of violence, not a book that praises it. Levithan adds:

> We knew because Suzanne had written *The Underland Chronicles* that she wasn't gonna be exploitative. We knew that the violence was there as a critique of violence and so because of that, what would've been scary subject matter in the hands of another author, we really trusted Suzanne to deal with it responsibly and we knew that if there was gonna be violence, there was gonna be violence for a reason. ("Gamemaker")

Teen and child soldiers are not glorified in the series, but undergo trauma throughout the battles and long after, emphasizing the ultimate destructiveness of war today.

As the series reflects our world, from the wasteful luxury of the American lifestyle to the callousness, it cries out for social change. In a world of desensitization to violence, it's a commentary on who we're becoming as a people, and how other nations are growing to see us.

At the same time, the series offers deep historical references from Shakespeare's plays and the time of Caesar: Characters Enobaria and Octavia hail from *Antony and Cleopatra*; Coriolanus Snow from his namesake play; and Brutus, Caesar Flickerman, Cato, Cinna, Claudius Templesmith, Flavius, Messalla, Portia, and Purnia from *Julius Caesar*. Collins saw Katniss as a modern day Theseus or Spartacus, the gladiator condemned to die in the Roman arena who finally led a revolution against the greedy Capitol.

It's also a story about storytelling, as Katniss makes herself into the Mockingjay and sings of a better future. The movie adaptation, especially, has a subplot about Seneca Crane, the twisty-bearded Gamemakers who is executed for telling too good a story. But even as Haymitch protests that this is all just a television show, Collins reminds us that it's far more.

Why is the trilogy such a success? Is it the nonstop first person immediacy?

The serious themes? The glimpse of a horrific, yet all-too-possible future? All this and more. This book explores the many genres and messages covered by *The Hunger Games* series: That hunger is not a game, that a single courageous voice can topple a dictator. War is the ultimate evil, and the death of innocents the worst crime of all. By making us care about Katniss and her friends, Collins opens our eyes to today's most powerful issues. And that's the real power of *The Hunger Games* today.

KATNISS THE REALITY TV STAR
Reflection in a Plastic Mirror

"I was channel surfing between reality TV programming and actual war coverage when Katniss's story came to me," Suzanne Collins comments. "One night I'm sitting there flipping around and on one channel there's a group of young people competing for, I don't know, money maybe? And on the next, there's a group of young people fighting an actual war. And I was tired, and the lines began to blur in this very unsettling way, and I thought of this story" ("Conversation"). In *The Hunger Games* trilogy, Katniss survives by playing the part she's been assigned, competing on the public screen to win her audience's support as star-crossed lover and political figurehead. But as she's forced to smile for the camera and the Capitol's frivolous, pleasure-seeking citizens, Panem with its Hunger Games begins to mirror another world – ours. This isn't just a dystopian future; it's the dystopia of present-day America.

From the first moment of Katniss's visit to the Capitol, she's stunned by its superficial society. Each person owns more clothes, shoes, wigs, and makeup than any ten people of her district. They swallow brightly colored pills with their morning coffee, reminiscent of our many drugs and vitamins. And they practice social bulimia, throwing up at feasts to make room for more, as the other towns starve. Katniss is appalled at the waste.

Embarking from her first train ride, Katniss appears much like a foreigner from a developing country. She gazes awestruck at the skyscrapers, glistening cars, and garishly dressed people who have clearly never gone hungry. The colors especially stand out for her: pinks, greens, and yellows impossible in nature, foreign to the forest-dwelling huntress. She has entered another world. Once within it, she longs to ride up and down on the glass elevator and marvels at the abundance of elegant food. The shower has a hundred settings of massage, strange soaps, and warm air. And there's far too much light to see the stars.

Effie Trinket, guide to this world, condescends to Katniss and Peeta, dwelling on their table manners and the "barbarism" of their district (*HG* 74). She believes that anyone without a Capitol upbringing is sadly lacking.

America today, of course, is often less than kind towards those who can't speak the language or blend in. As Katniss endures the criticism, she in turn considers how obtuse Effie is: her "civilized" society is preparing the new tributes for slaughter, all for a few episodes of live television. The Gamemakers, too, consider tributes beneath notice, and they ignore Katniss's demonstration of her combat skills in favor of stuffing themselves. When she shoots their dinner in true barbaric fashion, she also reveals their spoiled behavior, these bureaucrats who shrug off the death of others as entertainment.

Capitol citizens appear wasteful and glutinous, especially to the near-starving Katniss. With one meal, she calculates how much hunting and gathering she would have to do to afford the chicken in orange sauce, even with thrifty substitutions. She's disturbed by how much the people take for granted. The true horror comes at the *Catching Fire* banquet held in honor of the new victors, when she discovers gluttony beyond her imagining. Everyone is expected to stuff themselves, vomit, and stuff themselves again. Delicate glasses of clear liquid are even provided for the purpose. Peeta condemns the citizens with horror, while Katniss can only think of the emaciated children back home. But American readers can see a parallel in bulimics, people who can afford to throw away food, binge and purge from dieting, and waste more meals than some people ever see.

While the Capitol citizens color their hair pink and green, dye their skin, and glory in cosmetic surgery, their fashions aren't much more extreme than those of Americans today. Katniss's stylists want to augment her breasts to make her more attractive once she's a star – a common practice in Hollywood. Her descriptions of Capitol citizens blowing up their lips and tattooing themselves with cult symbols (like the mockingjay) are popular in our own culture, as is their obsession with looking youthful. "Do they really have no idea how freakish they look to the rest of us?" Katniss wonders (*CF* 49). For those struggling for food and warmth, our garish lipstick, hair dyes, and unnecessary surgeries must seem ridiculous indeed, as we design exotic fashions out of boredom and waste money on luxuries so decadent they're outlandish. Our reality shows are filled with divas obsessing over their hair colors or the source of their next million. The first episode of *The Real Housewives of New Jersey* introduced Teresa, who loves shopping for her new multi-million dollar dream home. On *The Real Housewives of Atlanta*, Shereé got nearly two million dollars in cash and property in her divorce. When she didn't receive alimony, she appealed to the Supreme Court of Georgia, explaining that she had few job skills and needed help to support herself and her children. Ramona on *The Real Housewives of New York City* sells her own line of jewelry through the Home Shopping Network and developed the skin care line, TruRenewal, while her fellow housewife Heather owns the shapewear business, Yummie Tummie. These "Real Housewives" our networks show off to the world are often spoiled, squabbling princesses with millions to spend on frivolous pet projects. Can they really spend so much on jeweled dog collars and big screen TVs while the world goes hungry?

Katniss's prep team shaves off all her body hair and bathes her over and over, removing her objectionable "third-world" origins. Only her hairstyle gets to stay (though team members don't say "exotic primitive craftsmanship," they're likely thinking it). Katniss sees her groomed self as alien – a stranger in the mirror. The prep team themselves are notable for their alien nature, with odd hair colors, fashion affectations, and even strange accents. Katniss sees them as incomprehensible twittering birds. Their entire purpose for being – to make Katniss look appealing – is incomprehensible to her. In her life, she ignores all unnecessary luxuries in favor of simple survival. Critic Ned Vizzini, in his essay "Reality Hunger," explains, "A world like the Capitol, where food can appear at the touch of a button and image is everything, does not seem real to Katniss, and *realness* – real emotion, real resolve, real fire – is at the heart of *The Hunger Games*" (83).

Katniss expects to be paraded around wearing a miner's getup or coal dust – not because this is who she is, but because it's how the Capitol views her district. She might as well be Miss Wisconsin, carrying a cutout of her state or a giant cheese. However, her stylist, Cinna, chooses to surround her with flame. Although this fire, like her later symbol of the Mockingjay, is an artificial construct, both echo the natural power inside Katniss, her strength and will for survival. "We've literally outshone them all," Katniss thinks after her dazzling display (*HG* 72). But what outshines the other tributes is Katniss's honest, blunt love for her family that fuels her determination.

The Miss America-style interviews, with high-heeled shoes, groomed nails, and heavy makeup, all mirror the pageantry of our culture – even among children. *Toddlers & Tiaras*, an American reality series, shows kindergarteners and two-year-olds wearing fake eyelashes, spray tans, and swimwear as they compete in "glitz" beauty pageants that judge their artificial, doll-like beauty. The names of various pageants, such as "America's Trezured Dollz" or "Precious Moments Pageant" only add to the stereotype. And it is just such a competition in which Katniss is trapped. To the Capitol, Katniss is not meant to be strong or independent – only appealing in a jeweled gown. She must giggle and smile to charm sponsors, who like her best when Peeta's proclaimed affection makes her look "weak" (as Katniss puts it) – a word Haymitch considers equivalent to "desirable" (*HG* 135). She is remade and objectified, perched on a stool as a lovely passive model for the audience to gape at. Beside her in line sit Rue, dressed as a tiny gossamer fairy, and Glimmer in a see-through golden gown looking "provocative" (*HG* 125). On *Toddlers and Tiaras*, tiny competitors must present giant, fixed smiles, must blow kisses and flirt. Backstage, however, many have tantrums at the pressure of their parents' expectations, at the endless practice, at the irritating beauty treatments. Katniss, in her high heels and jeweled gowns, must perform in the same way. And Katniss certainly has her tantrums before Cinna and Effie, as she cries for hours and tears apart her room. With this, Collins portrays the misery of beauty pageants, since inside, Katniss feels murderous.

Katniss must also adopt an artificial persona – a platform to make viewers care for her. Adrianne Curry, former contestant on *America's Next Top Model,* gives advice to potential contestants that mirrors Haymitch's and Cinna's advice to Katniss. Curry suggests that aspirants find a persona like "drama queen" or "girl next door" or just be natural: "Just be yourself, and if being yourself isn't interesting, make up a character. . . . Everyone loves the bitch. Everyone loves the underdog. Everyone loves the diva" (Robinson 229). Katniss attempts being spunky or sexy or sweet, but the forthright girl fails at all these. Only when Cinna coaches her to be herself and answer questions as if talking to a friend does she succeed. The audience comes to love her because of her lack of artifice. She shares a truth they find unusually appealing in the world of superficiality in which they exist. She's a genuine heroine, one who sacrificed herself for her young sister, one who hunts to survive, one who is honestly shocked when Peeta declares his love for her. And as such, she appeals to them and to us. "*The Hunger Games* presents us with the kind of hero that not only Panem but America likes best: the reluctant one, unexpectedly brilliant when challenged and then, once famous, desirous of a simpler life," says Vizzini (84).

The citizens of the Capitol, so used to their superficial lives, crave novelty, but they also crave genuineness. And there is nothing more genuine than a real fight to survive, fought by (mostly) guileless children from the more primitive districts. Nely Galan, creator of *The Swan,* explains, "Ultimately, the stars of reality TV are real people. I find it fascinating, because we spend so many years idolizing celebrities, and now real people get a shot at it" (Robinson 85). Such is the appeal of allegedly unscripted television. When Peeta describes on television what the Games are truly like, there's a hush across the room, as everyone is entranced by the tale of unadulterated terror and the fight for survival. Suzanne Collins notes:

> The Hunger Games is a reality television program. An extreme one, but that's what it is. And while I think some of those shows can succeed on different levels, there's also the voyeuristic thrill, watching, people being humiliated or brought to tears or suffering physically. And that's what I find very disturbing. There's this potential for desensitizing the audience so that when they see real tragedy playing out on the news, it doesn't have the impact it should. It all just blurs into one program. (Hudson)

While there are parallels with celebrity makeover shows, wedding shows, and talent competitions, the Hunger Games themselves are closest to *Survivor.* As Matthew Robinson describes the show in his book on reality television, contestants are "dumped into a remote location and made to fend for themselves . . . . If having no food, water, or shelter wasn't bad enough, these 'survivors' also have to figure out how to connive and manipulate one another in order to survive the voting-off ceremony at each week's tribal council. Oh yeah, and sometimes they also have to eat rats" (173). The disturbing part as the contestants suffer through starvation and injury in fetching bikinis is that their scenario is no more real than the environment of the Hunger Games: they are trapped on their island purely to entertain the masses with their misery.

Mitchell Olson, a contestant on *Survivor: Australia,* revealed that all the laughter and campfire sing-alongs got edited out: "I guess because it's not as dramatic – it doesn't show us being stressed out and starving" (Robinson 182). This echoes Katniss's dismay as the Gamemakers throw in firestorms and traps just to raise the level of action. Granted, *Survivor* is more likely to have challenges of racing through an obstacle course to collect puzzle pieces than fleeing a firestorm. But even tests depending on teamwork feature cameras poised to catch the complaints and frustration. Scandal, tears, arguments, and recriminations are the lifeblood of reality shows, in which contestants are urged to share their frustration with viewers, to blame other contestants, to have tantrums onscreen. Even on this small scale, contestants undeniably suffer for viewers' amusement. "Evoking emotion from the casting department is the name of the game, so do whatever you can to up the tearjerker factor," Robinson advises (39). Whether deaths in the Hunger Games or momentary misery, the reality show must have drama.

One common protest against reality TV is its total lack of privacy for contestants. Intimate conversations and romances have been broadcast on national TV, often against the participants' wishes (Biltereyst 93). In this way, Katniss's emotional talks with Peeta are offered to the camera in a performance she must knowingly put on for the masses. The Game makes even emotion artificial, as Katniss gives Peeta long, lingering kisses to entertain the cameras and sponsors. It's entertainment, and she knows her lines. She who is most entertaining will live longest, a rule in our society of *American Idol* and Miss America, as well as in Katniss's. While the sponsors' products don't come with brand names, they almost could, reminding viewers that Katniss survived by using Acme burn cream or Johnson's sleeping bags. The sponsors choose which tribute to support based on beauty and appeal, like today's advertisers choosing a spokesmodel.

A leading newspaper in Greece claimed that reality TV would bring to the surface of society the most repulsive and deplorable characteristics of human nature (Biltereyst 97). In the Hunger Games, these are evident in the

Career Tributes, whom Katniss describes as "overly vicious," and the "Capitol's lapdogs" (*HG* 161). A past tribute turned cannibal in the games, and even gentle Peeta resolves to kill other children to defend himself. Reality TV is fundamentally exploitative, as "the programme-makers exploit their subjects through 'manipulation' and editorial control, or the participants exploit the programmer in an entrepreneurial bid for media exposure" (Holmes 111). While Katniss is tortured for the entertainment of the masses, the Career Tributes try to exploit the Games in return, to become proficient killers in return for wealth and fame. Only in the final book do we discover that many media darlings of the Games like Finnick are still exploited, forced to be a source of entertainment and prostitution for the Capitol.

Reality shows, "generate only a *faux* community, one that obliterates trust" (Cavender 169). These echo President George W. Bush's Homeland Security programs, which, like the policies of Panem, allowed the government to eavesdrop their citizens without warrants. Being in such an environment encourages betrayal and blame-shifting, as citizens fear to say what they really think. Katniss always knows someone is watching. Similarly, the Hunger Games tributes know they cannot work together, that any alliances must end with destroying one another. While Katniss's humanity prevails over the rules and she bonds with Rue, she fears most of all the threat they will be left until the end and forced to turn on each other. This is indeed the worst side of humanity, not its best.

Months after their triumphs, reality TV contestants appear on talk shows, in newspapers, and on the Web, informing bored fans about their lives. In the second book, Katniss and Peeta have the Victory Tour, a series of press events meant to entertain the masses and promote the Capitol's agenda. But Katniss finds it hard to stay herself as she slips into the celebrity persona the Capitol demands. Once more she's buffed and groomed, stuffed into perfectly designed outfits. Her romance with Peeta is owned and managed by the public, not by her. When their engagement, too, is staged, she models wedding dresses for her fans, who will log in to vote on her gown like so many *American Idol* groupies.

In *Catching Fire*, it's revealed that Katniss is expected to develop a "talent," as if her connection with Miss America wasn't clear enough already. Flower arranging and playing instruments are common choices. Peeta starts painting, a hobby for the rich. But Katniss's only "talents" are singing, which is too personal, and hunting, which doesn't count (if shooting a painted target won't make the cut, presumably Katniss is supposed to cultivate a purely frivolous art in keeping with Capitol pursuits, rather than a practical or violent hobby). Katniss, worthless at frivolous time-wasting, has Cinna help her pretend she designs clothing, while Peeta paints the Hunger Games, in a move both rebellious and therapeutic. These required talents not only reflect the foolishness of the Capitol, but also the "accomplishments" ladies of quality once learned, like dancing, foreign languages, and embroidery. They were designed to fill a day and add to one's refinement, rather than being useful chores to bring in money (like laundry or weaving). They were the opposite of work, serious education, or higher thought, and were used to keep ladies useless and decorative, just as Katniss the spokesmodel becomes. They are also a form of Bread and Circuses, ensuring that those with fame and success are too contented to question the government.

In *Mockingjay*, former Head Gamemaker Plutarch Heavensbee describes the Capitol's obsession with "*Panem et Circenses*" (Bread and Circuses) (*MJ* 223). This was a Roman concept, for the Capitol itself is a mirror of Rome, the founder of Western civilization's gluttony. With plenty of "Bread and Circuses" – food and entertainment – the citizens are kept spoiled and debauched, caring nothing for politics or the deprivation of others. The founders of Panem may have named the world after this philosophy (and if the Capitol is defined by bread, the rest of Panem and the Hunger Games themselves are certainly defined by its lack). Sadly, we Americans are also living in a world of bread and circuses, filled with more entertainment channels than news. We are kept amused, distracted, fed to the point of being overfed. We can obsess like reality shows' "Real Housewives" over new cars we must have and exotic fashions we must design. But at its base, this lifestyle is frivolous, wasteful, and thoroughly artificial. Perhaps that is part of what Suzanne Collins wants us to remember. In an interview, she explains that she employed the dystopian setting of her novels to explore "the power of television and how it's used to influence our lives" (Hudson).

The Games themselves reflect this, fought as they are in a completely synthetic environment. When Katniss enters the arena, its artificiality is emphasized in every moment. The weather and temperature are designed to kill contestants. The very wasps and jays have been artificially bred to hurt people, leaving nature a deadly snare. As Elizabeth Rees says, "Nothing in Katniss's previous experience can prepare her for the calculated, psychologically brutal nature of the Gamemakers' tricks and traps" (47). Backpacks and night-vision goggles scattered for the tributes, spontaneous "feasts," and sponsor gifts are thrown in to add to the spice, mimicking the rewards on shows like *Survivor*. And like *Survivor*, every dramatic moment must be played for the camera. As television critic Christopher Dunkley points out, "the phrase 'reality television'. . . is ultimately silly because . . . it places groups of people desperate for fame in the most contrived and artificial situations" (24). The golden Cornucopia, overflowing with deadly weapons, is the perfect symbol of the Games.

Katniss and her friend Rue, each named for the natural environment they embody, succeed using the skills they learned out in the country: Rue's knowledge of berries and wasp sting remedies, Katniss's hunting skills and plant lore. Even Peeta's camouflage, as he paints himself into the natural environment and becomes part of it, is essential to keep him alive. Their lifestyle of simplicity and economy contrasts with the Capitol's lifestyle at every turn. As Katniss reflects, she and Rue are used to living in nature, used to going hungry, so they're better prepared for this survival course than the Career Tributes, who pile up supplies from the artificial Cornucopia, building a pyramid of crates and land mines as Rue and Katniss fade silently into the trees. Finally, Katniss, who despises artificiality, blows up the pyramid of supplies, using – apples! "*Let the Seventy-fourth Hunger Games begin*," she thinks gleefully, committing to take the Careers down, rather than just survive (*HG* 226, italics in original). Deprived of their unfair stockpile of supplies, the Careers must fight her on an equal footing. In fact, they must now suffer through the Hunger Games as she has been, rather than lording over them. And as a girl so attuned with nature, Katniss has a chance of winning.

Running off into the forest and staying there is Katniss's great fantasy through the misery of her life; it's her image of Eden. It's also an American fantasy, as literature by James Fennimore Cooper, Washington Irving, and Henry David Thoreau focuses on the retreat into the forest, the quest for a return to nature. It offers simplicity, endless bounty, and safety from the agendas of others. But the forest remains a fantasy or only a momentary sanctuary where Katniss can slip off with Gale or can remember her father. She is imprisoned in one Game, then a second, and then in the ultimate Game of the snare-filled Capitol.

The Quarter Quell arena offers an environment shaped like a clock, whose deadly traps switch on and off artificially. Peeta envisions it ticking away his life, with "every hour promising some new horror" (*MJ* 22). There are no mockingjays here, only jabberjays who torture Katniss with the cries of her loved ones. The monkeys are mutated monsters, it rains blood, and poisoned fog shrouds the land. Ever present are the force fields, a teasing, deadly reminder of the real world just beyond. This time, however, the participants use the arena's artificial nature to crack it open and escape, breaking through the phoniness and destroying it. The setup of the Games reminds Katniss that there are real people torturing her for entertainment, that every child's death must be laid at their feet. The enemy of *Catching Fire* is not the survival course but frigid, calculating President Snow.

After escaping from the second arena, Katniss arrives at District 13, an even more artificial environment than the Capitol. Indeed, as critic Elizabeth M. Rees notes, "The district proves to be a distorted mirror image of the Capitol itself" (55). For while the Capitol's citizens disdain nature in favor of entertainment, District 13 is all utilitarian and grey. The Capitol glorifies in waste and excess; District 13 forbids alcohol, drugs, and indulgence. Everything is carefully controlled, from measured food portions to the schedules tattooed on each forearm until the allotted bath time. Katniss, once again miserable, finds herself seeking nature in small ways, begging to hunt for fresh food and arranging to keep Prim's cat.

Worse yet, she must be the Mockingjay, television personality. The rebels try to film Katniss on a sound stage, a faux bloody bandage on her arm and a scripted slogan on her lips. It fails. Only the genuine Katniss – grieving, loving, sacrificing – can charm her followers. When she dances at Finnick's wedding, recovers in a hospital bed, and trains for action, all her reactions are captured for the camera. She must struggle to identify her own needs, buried as they are beneath everyone's desire to use her. Vizzini says, "She is forced to consider how much of her persona is real and how much is fashioned by her many handlers, from Cinna to Haymitch to President Coin – all of whom do not end up well" (84). At last, absent of her will, Katniss's hand writes the demand, "*I KILL SNOW*" (*M* 38, caps and italics in orig.). With most of her spirit buried in others' needs, Katniss finds revenge still flickers within.

Assigned to the Star Squad, Katniss is trapped in a unit used for publicity shots. When her staged battles prove uninteresting on camera, a real fight is set up against Capitol booby-traps, in a mission that is designed to serve as a photo shoot, so much so that Katniss's camera director, Cressida, is the one to cry, "Action!" (*MJ* 275). However, an unexpected trap kills Katniss's commander, shattering the photo-shoot atmosphere. Real smoke and blood replace the special effects, and the staged scene turns very ugly. In this moment, Katniss takes charge through the deception she believes she has slowly come to master. Lying to the squad about a secret mission, she leads them, now a general not a pawn, as they fight on. Her buried agenda takes over and this core of will, which has simmered beneath orders and agendas, leads them all the way to the President's mansion. The squad's survivors later reveal that they saw through her lie but wanted to follow her anyway, their Mockingjay. All the fakery for the camera has become truth.

The violence ends ironically. Katniss seems to yield to the new President Coin's demands, to do all she must to fire the last shot of the war. But this shot (in the form of an arrow) is aimed at Coin, the true manipulator, the one who murders children to steal popular opinion about the war. And Katniss rebels at last, firing her final shot at the ultimate deceiver. The former Mockingjay heals from the war only when she settles in her old district, caring for the dead and memorializing the truth of their lives in a book. She retires from all forms of media attention, keeping only her true friends Peeta and Haymitch. She returns to hunting. District 12, no longer a dangerous coalmine, becomes an agrarian culture, where children laugh and play in a meadow. By returning to nature, Katniss can return to simple village life, disdaining forever the superficial world of the Capitol. For her, there is a greater truth in the forest.

We in America still dwell among the artificial lights, wastefulness, and constant entertainment filling our screens. We prefer to watch others suffer and strive than to do so ourselves. Collins warns us that an obsession with bread and circuses can lead to a dark future of apathy and callousness regarding others' suffering, something we already see in American citizens as they laugh at people's misery on *Fear Factor* or *Survivor*. Worse yet, a lifetime of deprivation for those less fortunate can soon turn to anger and revolution. Thus, Collins shows us the potential downfall of corporate America, in danger of being destroyed by the nations we've oppressed and ignored as we barely make it off our couches to protest. Our obsession with luxury has turned to blindness and a startlingly naïve political reality compared with those living in other countries. It's time, Collins reminds us, that we start paying attention to the world, becoming part of it rather than just watching. The important thing is knowing where to draw the line between entertainment and reality.

KATNISS THE REVOLUTIONARY
A Look at Dystopian Literature

"Telling a story in a futuristic world gives you this freedom to explore things that bother you in contemporary times," Suzanne Collins explains. For her, these are "issues like the vast discrepancy of wealth, the power of television and how it's used to influence our lives, the possibility that the government could use hunger as a weapon, and...the issue of war" (Hudson). In her trilogy, she crafts a world that's most disturbing because of its ugly parallels with our own: children starve, the government spies on its citizens, rewritten history airs on television. Like many of the great dystopian authors, Collins reveals the injustice and cruelty of those in power as Katniss discovers the futility and slender hope offered by revolution.

Dystopia

There are countless classic dystopian novels, from adult works by Kurt Vonnegut and Ray Bradbury to the younger *The Giver* or *Books of Ember*. But *The Hunger Games* and its decade have brought a new renaissance of dystopias, like Michael Grant's *Gone* series or Susan Beth Pfeiffer's *Life As We Knew It*.

Why are these all arriving now? With headlines on global warming, terrorism, nuclear tests, worldwide economic distress, and wars in Afghanistan and Iraq, people feel uneasy. After 9/11 and the flood in New Orleans, readers have discovered the precarious nature of our society and the uncertainty of what is to come. "Western civilization used to produce literary utopias, but in the past century of world wars, financial panics, murderous totalitarian regimes and nuclear threat, dystopias have outnumbered sunny projections by several orders of magnitude," comments critic Brian Bethune in his article "Dystopia Now."

When we explore the dark mirror of ourselves, America-that-could-be, we explore the dark impulses of humanity and our worst fears. Some psychologists compare this to exposure therapy, a way to address our fears bit by bit and so become comfortable with them. For readers, the world of what if's is awfully appealing. Panem is not our world, but a possible future, post-apocalypse and post-democracy. "We like to be scared of things that are not real. The idea that we're watching or reading things that are completely outlandish or impossible or realty dire helps us cope with what *is*," comments Karen Springen in her own *Publishers Weekly* article on dystopias. We can feel safe because it's fiction and because our world is less horrific than the one on the page. Through reading, we can confront fears of violence, persecution, and abuse, and battle through them beside the main character.

People in District Twelve suffer through public floggings and work in the dangerous mines, where accidents are commonplace. In District Eleven, a retarded child is executed for keeping a toy. Children routinely die of starvation, trapped behind a barbed wire fence. Workers are forbidden to keep the food they grow or coal they mine. However, the most chilling part is knowing these things happen on earth today. Collins explains:

> The sociopolitical overtones of *The Hunger Games* were very intentionally created to characterize current and past world events, including the use of hunger as a weapon to control populations. Tyrannical governments have also used the techniques of geographical containment of certain populations, as well as the nearly complete elimination of the rights of the individual. (Blasingame)

The Hunger Games are like a smaller concentration camp, compared to the larger ones known as the districts. People are condemned to both to suffer for the crimes of their ancestors. The electrified fences, the starvation and rationing, the people's utter helplessness when brutal taskmasters and soldiers arrive all echo our darkest moments in history. Though hidden in fiction, the trilogy carries a fervent plea for compassion and the repair of a shattered world.

LIFE IN *1984*

The novel *1984* is one of the world's most famous dystopian works and a favorite of Suzanne Collins's. The mysterious and unseen Big Brother, head of the Party, rules all aspects of citizens' lives. Televisions and cameras watch every room, and even silently resenting the government is prosecutable as a "thoughtcrime." The protagonist, Winston Smith, works for Big Brother, rewriting old newspaper articles to reflect the new version of history. Every moment, he must guard his expressions, pledge loyalty to Big Brother, control his very thoughts. At last, one day he can't take it anymore, and in his diary, his hand independently writes "DOWN WITH BIG BROTHER" (Orwell 20).

Katniss too follows orders in the Capitol and then District Thirteen until she can't bear the constant restrictions over every aspect of her life. Bath times, meal times, work times: all are regulated and even tattooed on her arm. At last, absent of her will, Katniss's hand writes the demand, "*I KILL SNOW*" (*MJ* 38, caps and italics in orig.). With most of her choices taken from her, Katniss finds revenge still flickers within.

Like Big Brother, President Snow's government controls the media and distributes disinformation to promote its agenda. The government spies on its people, with tapped phones, spy cameras, and the infamous jabberjays. Television watching is mandatory, for how else can the government be truly totalitarian, without controlling all means of entertainment and communication? Of course, its historical footage of the smoking remains of District Thirteen and its carefully edited interviews are fake history laden with propaganda, like Winston's revisions.

Only in the forest can Katniss find sanctuary. However, she discovers that Snow's hovercraft and cameras even operate there. The image of constant surveillance is popular in dystopian fiction. In *Divergent* and *Uglies*, adults monitor all aspects of teens' lives, including their thoughts and emotions. Teens learn to beat the system and lie, for those who are independent thinkers will be killed.

In *1984*, Winston Smith seeks out similar places where he won't be observed. After the enticing Julia gives him a piece of paper that says "I Love You," they run away from the cameras to be together deep in the woods. They finally start meeting in a "shabby little room" that echoes Katniss's abandoned house by the lake (Orwell 143). However, like Katniss when she kisses Gale in the meadow, Smith is always being watched.

In both stories, any illusion of freedom or safety is a lie. The Capitol rigs the Hunger Games drawings so the children of victors are chosen, for the extra drama of it. And the rules of the Game itself change to add excitement for the viewers and pain for those trapped within it. Those at the Capitol break their own rules when it pleases them, failing to deliver District Twelve's rightful rewards for Peeta and Katniss's winning the Hunger Games. Even the tesserae grain that the children buy with their lives doesn't always arrive in *Catching Fire*.

Corruption is heavy in District Twelve – there's a thriving black market, and the officials look the other way for crimes like poaching. The mayor and most of the other officials even buy Katniss's illegal gleanings. The "electrified fence" around District Twelve relies on an empty threat, as there's rarely any electricity. In this situation, Katniss learns the fine line of deception she must walk – selling strawberries at the mayor's back door and even selling meat to Peacekeepers, but not parading a deer or even a bow through town.

Living in such a dishonest place, Katniss has quickly learned the skills of deception herself. "I learned to hold my tongue and to turn my features into an indifferent mask so that no one could ever read my thoughts," she explains (*HG* 6). She brings in her kills after dark and doesn't talk treason where anyone can hear her. In *Catching Fire,* she hides her injuries from the latest poaching trip and laughs with Peeta and Haymitch, all for the benefit of Capitol security. She must treat Gale as her "cousin" to maintain her public romance with Peeta. Every moment, she remembers she's being observed. And of course, she must pretend to be delirious in love – a silly schoolgirl, not a revolutionary.

Suzanne Collins notes:

> The interesting thing about Katniss is when the story begins, she doesn't have much political awareness…And so she is struggling to put things together as she goes through the series, and it's quite difficult, because no one seems to think it's in their interest to educate her…Even though hers is an extreme case, I think all of us have to work to figure out what's going on. (Hudson)

Indeed, Katniss must question all that television programs and government schools have taught her about history, geography, politics, for much of it is false. At the story's beginning, she accepts that District Thirteen is a myth, that no one can oppose the Capitol and that survival is enough. She fails to save a rebel girl, who is turned into an Avox as punishment. But after winning her first Games by outsmarting the Capitol, she begins to question the Capitol's complete power and see the cracks within.

Katniss's power comes from compassion, a refusal to let the Capitol take her humanity. "We're gonna use innocent children as sacrificial lambs for our own spectacle. I mean, there's nothing more cynical than that. And yet, she finds humanity in the face of an inhuman situation," director Gary Ross reports ("Conversation"). Katniss frames Rue in flowers, reminding viewers that she and her friend are people, not sources of entertainment. She is rewarded with bread from Rue's district and rescue from Thresh, as they too, begin to treat her as a friend. Fire catches. So does kindness.

However, as with Katniss, Winston Smith finds his compassion terribly tested. He is arrested for his thoughtcrimes and tortured with his worst fear – rats – in order to remake him as someone loyal to the Party. When they strap a wire cage of rats to his face, he finally screams, "Do it to Julia! Not me!" (Orwell 300). The torture has been so severe that it has turned his love into hatred and fear. The humanity Katniss so desperately clings to in the Games has been taken from him. When they finally release Winston, he has come to worship Big Brother with a fanatical devotion. After betraying Julia, he cannot find his way back to loving her.

One of Snow's cruelest acts is his brainwashing of Peeta. With the hybrid tracker jacker venom, the Capitol fills his memories with confusion and doubt until memories of the terror and romance of the Games are twisted into pain and mistrust. Afterwards, Peeta returns to Katniss. In one creepy moment, mutts released through the sewers begin to whisper Katniss's name…and then

Peeta does as well. Katniss draws her bow and nearly shoots him, certain he will turn on her in moments. The government has turned the teens' innocent, genuine love into something vicious and corrupt, in the ultimate destruction of personal freedom. It takes the entire book for them to find their way through the guilt and anguish of the war and finally be together. "Both *The Hunger Games* and *Nineteen Eighty-Four* pit the power of hate versus the power of love," notes critic Mary Borsellino. While hate triumphs in the latter, *The Hunger Games* "ultimately insists that love is strong enough to survive through the horrors placed before it" (31).

HOBBES AND *LORD OF THE FLIES*

Collins often reads *1984* as well as *Lord of the Flies,* the story of a group of boys trapped together on an island who descend into savagery and kill one another (Jordan). Echoes of this violence and cruelty toward others appear throughout the *Hunger Games* Trilogy. But it has been a part of human nature for even longer than there have been dystopias. Jennifer Lawrence notes:

> It's a very sad story about this girl who's forced into doing this in this world where the rich watch children die as entertainment. It's gripping and it's urgent. It's a terrible world. It's actually not far off from reality. We live in a world where humanity is becoming so desensitized to violence and to tragedy that peoples' tragedy is our entertainment. We're obsessed with reality television and we get so numb to violence, tragedy, that it takes more to shock us, and more and more. It's not that science-fiction, if you think about it. (Mordsley, "Hunger Games Interview 4")

The philosopher Thomas Hobbes taught that life is "solitary, poore, nasty, brutish, and short" (84). For those in the districts, it is. Hobbes adds that humans are animalistic and cruel, capable of turning on each other and descending into chaos without a strong ruler. Thus, freedom must be sacrificed for the "safety of the people" (242). This provides an excuse for totalitarian government, to keep the people protected and well-behaved. "It is the Hobbesian solution of destroying liberty that has animated nearly all dystopias. Its unyielding logic drags us to a destination that we would avoid – if only it were not the only way out" (Halper and Muzzio 382). Human beings are savages, and only savage leaders can keep control.

In *Lord of the Flies* by William Golding, a group of schoolboys are shipwrecked on a desert island. The minute they have no adults to set boundaries, they quarrel for leadership. They finally begin to hunt and kill each other in their own brutal Hunger Games, battling with rocks and wooden spears.

Gone is little better. After the adults suddenly vanish, the teens and children set out to build a rational society. However, most children sit around apathetically – no one wants to work. "They were all like rats living in an abandoned house; they ate what they found, messed wherever they liked, and left things dirtier and more rundown than they had found them" (Grant 196). This description is all Hobbes could have predicted. Meanwhile, the rich school's charismatic leader Caine has secret powers, and his first move is to torture and render immobile anyone he fears could match his abilities. Bullies are appointed policemen. Soon, the teens are killing each other, egged on by the mysterious "Darkness" that dwells in a nearby mine. Before the first book has ended, the protagonist Sam is arming twelve-year-olds with machine guns because he fears that's the only way to stay safe.

Koushun Takami's *Battle Royale*, a Japanese novel and movie, is thought by many to have inspired Collins, though Collins comments that she's never read or seen it. In near-future totalitarian Japan, the government terrorizes the population by stranding a high school class on an island and forcing them to kill each other. Like Collins's work, this act is meant to punish the citizens by killing their children. However, as a class, the students already have relationships, casting a darker spin on the battle. In fact, like *Gone*, it becomes an exaggeration of high school itself. Bethune notes:

> *Battle Royale* involves a class full of teens who know each other well, with all the crushes, friendships and antagonisms that entails. If *The Hunger Games* is reality TV ratcheted to a madly logical end, *Battle Royale* is extreme high school: dating and death, indeed.

"Some critics have noted that the arena where the Hunger Games play out is a powerful symbol specifically because it stands in for that very public battleground of adolescence; the hallways of high school" (Seltzer 42). It's no accident that these Hobbsian battlegrounds take place between schoolchildren specifically. The hallways of high school indeed reflect the competition and cruelty that show off teens' strengths in a sort of battleground. There are the haves versus the have-nots, those who will win championships and those who will be left behind. Students are voted "most likely to succeed" and even have sponsors offering the best scholarships. There are many strategies for surviving both school and arena, from choosing alliances to being handsome and popular. Nonetheless, both arenas serve as reminders of youthful brutality.

Within Collins's Games, children murder each other without compassion. Even the wiser adult tributes of the second book, longtime friends and allies, savagely battle at the Cornucopia. "Have they all joined hands? Taken a vow of nonviolence?" Finnick asks Katniss sarcastically (*CF* 276). The tributes could indeed refuse to fight, sit on the ground, provide a passive spectacle instead of a bloodbath. Even the possible execution of all twenty-four candidates instead of certain death for twenty-three wouldn't be such a price for a chance to end the Games forever. Katniss and Peeta with their nightlock berries make that choice together. But in seventy-four years no other tributes have done this. A tiny selfish chance for survival becomes more important, and even the pacifist Peeta resolves to murder the other children for his own survival. Clearly, Suzanne Collins sees a trace of Hobbes's philosophy in human nature.

So too does President Snow. When it appears Katniss has died taking the Capitol, he appears on television, dismissing the rebels as unimportant: As Katniss explains, "He predicts a turning of the tide in the war, since the demoralized rebels have no one left to follow" (*MJ* 294). In Snow's philosophy, he might be overthrown by a stronger dictator, but not a chaotic mob that lack the direction to oppose him. Immediately, President Coin appears on television in response, identifying herself as the new leader, taking another step towards becoming the next Snow, even as she promises to protect the districts.

Watching all this, Katniss sees how tiny one revolutionary is against the horrors of human nature. Humanity will always turn on itself, always built nuclear weapons, always try to seize power, even when cooperation would serve it better. This knowledge sends her into despair in each book, as she realizes how little she can do to defy the system.

Absolute Power

George Orwell, author of *Animal Farm* and *1984*, often said, "Power corrupts. Absolute power corrupts absolutely." In other words, even a good person would become evil after gaining the unlimited power of presidency over Panem. In the novel *Animal Farm*, the pigs lead a revolution against the oppressive farmers, but soon they elevate themselves over their fellow animals and become indistinguishable from the masters they once hated. Though they win a revolution, nothing changes – the new leaders are just as bad. Here is the true danger of power, and it's one to which President Coin has succumbed even before her victory.

In *Catching Fire*, Katniss wonders if District Thirteen exists, why it's done nothing to help so many innocents. "Why do they leave us to live like this? With the hunger and the killing and the Games?" (*CF* 148). At this moment she realizes, prophetically, that they are no better than the Capitol. Ultimately, Coin, the revered leader of the revolution, stages a rescue with troops and helicopters. District Thirteen, though not a happy place, has sufficient food and shelter for its citizens. It welcomes the refugees…but there is a menacing aura to the place.

As critic Elizabeth M. Rees notes, "The district proves to be a distorted mirror image of the Capitol itself" (55). By rejecting everything the Capitol values, District Thirteen has embraced a different kind of dystopia. Both places separate themselves from nature, one with garish skyscrapers and cosmetic surgery; the other with the utilitarian underground bunkers. While Capitol citizens acquire closets of wigs and hold lavish banquets, in Thirteen, possessions and celebrations are considered selfish. Citizens there are strictly controlled and forbidden to waste, so much so that the prep team is confounded by the punishment for stealing bread. No one is allowed out except for mandatory military training. Everything, from the products of Katniss's hunting to her tube of skin ointment, must be shared among all.

The lack of tolerance for hoarding, the functional quarters and stark uniforms, the control over every aspect of life, and the insistence on total equality to the point of socialism echoes the former Soviet Union and its standard of living. The Russian Revolution of 1917 brought down the wasteful monarchy, who lived in luxury while peasants starved. New communist policies were meant to make everyone equal, sharing food, wealth, and technology among nobles and peasants alike. People worked for the good of everyone, not for their own personal profit. However, those leaders who imposed the communist system became totalitarian dictators. Joseph Stalin, who ruled from 1924 to 1953, killed millions of his own people in purges of anyone who might defy him. He was known for employing secret police and censoring free speech. Though his five-year plans improved technology, winning much of the Space Race for the USSR, his country was known for its lack of personal freedoms. Many readers consider *Animal Farm* itself to be an allegory for the Russian Revolution, as the revolution made things little better for the lowest class out in the countryside.

The first rebellion seventy-five years earlier and led by District Thirteen may have been a revolution along these lines, hoping to create a fairer world with everyone equal, instead of Capitol and districts. If so, they failed. The Capitol and Thirteen began a seventy-five year cold war, each aiming nuclear missiles at the other. While Thirteen could have become a source of protection and hope for its neighbors, it makes no effort (evident to the reader) to spread knowledge of its existence, let alone supplies. Its children are safe from the Hunger Games. As such, it and the Capitol come to resemble world superpowers, too concerned with creating deadly weapons to send food and aid to the their third world neighbors. Only when their war spills outwards into the districts do Thirteen and the Capitol send soldiers and medical teams to protect their own allies, as happened through numerous global conflicts during the Cold War. District Thirteen sits in isolation and secrecy for seventy-five years, until, mirroring their sterility and lack of change, their population falls. Only then do they welcome District Twelve.

Katniss's first indicator that something is seriously wrong is when she finds her former prep team shackled and abused on one of the lower levels. Just when Katniss has been agonizing over Peeta being tortured and kidnapped by President Snow, these innocents are likewise being cruelly treated. And like Peeta, they've been imprisoned to punish Katniss – they are tortured, partially for stealing bread, but more as a warning, like Gale's public whipping for poaching a turkey. Coin has already become the tyrant. Katniss quickly realizes that their mistreatment is a message from President Coin, that she is in control and can do what she likes with Katniss's friends. This has been the message that President Snow has always sent her, as he threatens Katniss's family, and bombs Katniss's district. When Katniss tries to warn Plutarch, he calmly replies that he's immune from harm, as he's crucial to Coin's war effort. Katniss replies, "The tributes were necessary to the Games, too. Until they weren't" (*MJ* 51). After fighting through two Games, she's learned that those in charge can always change the rules.

When she takes power, Coin reveals her true monstrosity. Ordering executions and scapegoating, she repeats Snow's agenda. Career Tributes and even prep teams are executed. Naïve, bubble-headed Effie Trinket only survives because she's labeled a rebel. Worst of all, she murders a group of Capitol children, enticing them with silver parachutes that carry a round of bombs, then a second round, to kill not only the children but their rescuers. It is President Snow who must reveal this to a grieving but still somewhat naïve Katniss. He understands Coin because their quests for total power are identical. The rulers may change, but the most powerless, society's children, will always be victims.

Coin imprisons Snow in his beautiful rose gardens, and Katniss realizes it's to set a precedent: If Coin is deposed in the future, it will be understood that presidents are entitled to special treatment. Clearly President Coin realizes that this revolution may be followed by another as history repeats. In her ultimate ruling, Coin wishes to reinstate the Hunger Games, forcing children to atone for the wrongs of the Capitol. As the scent of Snow's last rose wafts through the room, Katniss wonders how similar the meeting was that created the Games, seventy-five years before. This chilling moment shows Katniss that truly nothing has changed. "This is why we rebelled! Remember?" Peeta protests (*MJ* 370). But the rebels have become the overlords, punishing their new subjects. Nothing is different but the names of those in power.

Though Katniss executes Coin, life doesn't change all that much. First she is imprisoned while those in charge decide her fate. "Taking my life is the Capitol's privilege. Again," she thinks (*MJ* 375). Gale, now one of the ruling class, goes to work in District Two, perhaps supervising the Peacekeepers who once whipped him in the marketplace, perhaps designing more weapons for the future. Effie Trinket is still an organizer for the Capitol's spectacles. Plutarch becomes Secretary of Communications, airing the broadcasts he has created in all three books. If another war comes, he will find another role for Katniss. But until then, she's to be tucked out of the way.

Looking to the Future

"YA [young adult] authors are using the dystopian genre to grapple with the issues of today," says David Levithan, editorial director at Scholastic. "It's about improving the dystopia rather than throwing up your hands and saying, 'This is what we're fated to be'" (Springen). Science fiction authors are our modern philosophers, asking the hard questions about how we conduct our lives. They show us societies where the environment has been ruined or genetic disorders shorten peoples' lives. Some artificially assign careers or spouses to teens, exploring how such choices would change us as a people. Now Suzanne Collins has joined this debate, seeking to remind her readers that suffering isn't entertainment.

The world of dystopia is teen worries intensified, exploring career choices through the faction assignments in *Divergent* or adult responsibility in *Gone*. The Hobbesian world of brutality is only a mirror of high schools with their cliques and bullies.

> What feeds the teenager's appetite for global destruction? We think of children and adolescents as being interested only in anodyne, escapist fiction – but that's to forget what it's actually like to be a teenager. When you're that age, everything feels like the end of the world: every test and snub and class and audition and prom. Adults have been around the block a few times. Whether it's because we have more perspective or we're just jaded, nothing is that big a deal to us. But you need to tear down the entire planet to match what goes on in a teenager's interior universe. The apocalypse is where they live. (Grossman)

When Katniss settles in District Twelve again, she has come to realize that people can defy an evil dictator but never the evils of human nature. As critic and author Sarah Rees Brennan puts it, "There is no easy way to defeat the evil in the world of the Hunger Games. It is the evil inherent in all of us" (9).

Katniss has learned this lesson, so she stays far from the new government that Gale and Effie still serve. Plutarch Heavensbee cynically comments that after the horror of war fades, more violence will always come. But he finishes by quietly hoping that humanity has evolved beyond that point. Katniss resolves to make her own little corner of the world better, and to remind others of the consequences of war. She writes a book with Peeta, memorializing those who died to bring about a new society, and those who were victims of the old one. With the stories of her friends, like the stories of *The Hunger Games* trilogy, perhaps humanity can turn away from the violence and cruelty of our darker natures.

KATNISS THE CLASSIC WARRIOR WOMAN

Jennifer Lawrence commented: "I loved the futuristic Joan of Arc character of Katniss. ….the book speaks truly about our time – it's incredibly relevant" (Egan 22). Laura Miller of *Salon* adds that Collins has "given us a heroine preoccupied with duty and justice – a chaste archer like the virgin goddess of the hunt, Artemis." Artemis, a young huntress herself, was a guardian of children. She was the classic daddy's girl, as was her motherless half-sister Athena. In *Oresteia*, Athena famously utters, "There is no mother anywhere who gave me birth ... I am always for the male with all my heart, and strongly on my father's side" (Aeschylus 161).

> Athena dwindles to virginal maiden, goddess of Zeus's intelligence, in service of the male solar ego. She molds men into heroes, teaching them warfare, while she teaches the women crafts of the home…She has become a sexless defender of the patriarchy, as an extension of Zeus, no more. (Frankel, *From Girl to Goddess* 136-137)

Katniss likewise disdains her useless, childlike mother, focusing all her energy on taking her father's place and using his skills to feed the family. "I got my father's blood," she says dismissively when Peeta compliments her healing skills (*CF* 322). In the woods, she wears her father's hunting jacket, wields his bow, and consults his book of wisdom. Katniss is most often found displaying traditional "masculine qualities such as athleticism, independence, self-sufficiency, and a penchant for violence" (Lem and Hassel 118). She rejects Prim's tearful hug and refuses to cry herself as she departs for the Games since she doesn't want to show weakness. At the Capitol, she's determined not to bond with her fellow tributes, especially Peeta, and resents owing him debts for saving her life. Sentimentality is not an option. She approaches romance with the same detachment, uncertain how to make herself look vulnerable, romantic, or charming in the cave.

This defensive quality is a particular mark of the classic warrior woman. In Norse myth, Brunhilda was the best of Odin's warrior women, the Valkyries. After she breaks his laws, he curses her to lie sleeping in a ring of fire, waiting for a hero to come for her. Though she seems a helpless princess in a tower, the wording of the original story has a much different feel:

> Sigurth [the hero] went into the shield-tower, and saw that a man lay there sleeping with all his war-weapons. First he took the helm from his head, and then he saw that it was a woman. The mail-coat was as fast as if it had grown to the flesh. ("Sigrdrifumol" 388)

As she lies there sleeping, with rigid armor so thick she appears to be a boy, the image is not seduction but cold protectiveness.

Like all these mythic women, Katniss clings to her eternal virgin status well into teenagerhood. Her mother famously tells the press that Katniss is too young for a boyfriend at age sixteen, though some people in her district wed that young. Katniss's own hesitation is understandable. When Gale remarks that Katniss will choose whoever gives her the best chance to survive, he zeroes in on her personality. She's been preoccupied with staying alive, so much so that it defines her existence.

The warrior woman's natural defensiveness means she has difficulty opening herself to emotion and romance. When she finally does, she follows the classic pattern of her heroic sisters: Mu Lan, Atlanta, the hordes of Amazons and Valkyries.

> History gives us Boudicca, who led a rebellion against Rome; Queen Tomyris, defeater of Cyrus the Great; Artemisia, general of Xerxes; Joan of Arc, who liberated France and became a saint. In modern retellings she is Ellen Ripley of the *Alien* movies, Xena, Max Guevara of *Dark Angel*, Nikita, Lara Croft, Red Sonja, many superheroes like Wonder Woman and Elektra. (Frankel, *Buffy and the Heroine's Journey* 7)

Éowyn of *The Lord of the Rings*. Buffy the Vampire Slayer, defender of women. The list is endless. Young adult and children's fantasy also offers many warrior heroines: Annabeth Chase (admittedly, Athena's daughter) from *Percy Jackson*. Harry Crewe of *The Blue Sword*. Deryn Sharp from Scott Westerfeld's *Leviathan* series. Alanna of Trebond, Keladry of Mindelan, and Beka Cooper from Tamora Pierce's Tortall books. Other fantasy authors also have amazing fighting women: Sherwood Smith, Mercedes Lackey, Marion Zimmer Bradley, Frewin Jones, Jim C. Hines, Jane Yolen.

While the warrior woman may disguise herself as a boy and wield a sword, a distance weapon is a more common choice: Xena has her chakram, while goddess Hecate has a barbed whip. The Valkyries hurl spears and arrows, the Morrigan wields lightning magic, Durga of India has a discus. Isabelle in *The Mortal Instruments* has a whip of electrum. Most common are bows like the one seen in the Pixar movie *Brave*. *Percy Jackson*'s Annabeth has a bow, as do Birgitte Silverbow from *The Wheel of Time* series and Felicity in *The Gemma Doyle Trilogy*.

Bows symbolize turning thought into action, the tension between everyday life and spirituality. The bow can also be a sign of harmony between heaven and earth, reality and unworldliness, since its arrows arc from one realm to the other. Arrows, with their feathers and flight, also share symbolism with birds and their freedom of expression. In the Bible, arrows are used to conquer evil, particularly at God's command:

> God judges the righteous, and God is angry with the wicked every day. If he turn not, he will whet his sword; he has bent his bow, and made it ready. (Psalm 7: 11-12).
>
> And in your majesty ride prosperously because of truth and meekness and righteousness; and your right hand shall teach you terrible things. Your arrows are sharp in the heart of the king's enemies; by which the people fall under you. (Psalm 45: 4-5).

Katniss's bows go through a progressive evolution, matching her personality. Her first bows are a gift from her father, the expert woodsman. Carved with his expertise, they mean survival in the forest. Later, the Capitol training bow is awkward for Katniss, reflecting how uneasy she is displaying her secret skills for the Capitol judges. She has never used their exotic technology, but only the handcrafted tools of distant District Twelve. The bow in the arena is gleaming silver. Silver represents the feminine sphere: feminine moon and water magic. It suggests chastity, purity, and innocence, appropriate signs of the immature maiden on her quest. Medieval writers considered silver a symbol of purity that could shield one from different maladies and monsters, and indeed, the bow is Katniss's only defense.

Katniss is given her ultimate bow in *Mockingjay*. Black, with flaming and explosive arrows, this is a bow of death. Using it, she shoots hovercraft from the sky and becomes the girl on fire in truth. Receiving the black bow solidifies her confusion – it is a bow designed not to win sponsors or defend her life, but simply to kill. Worse, it is presented to her just as she decides to become the Mockingjay, giving her the choice to enter the war and kill other human beings. Black is of course death and mourning in Western culture – Katniss uses her bow to bring death but also to mourn the need for it. *Mockingjay* is characterized by Katniss's depression and emptiness, emotions associated with blackness. Caught in the depths of this state, mourning her sister's loss, she uses the bow to fire the "last shot of the war." At last her spiritual crisis is resolved as she executes the agent of all the death.

Back in District Twelve, Katniss returns to the simplicity of home and finds two of her father's bows. No longer a killer, she is a hunter again, and armed with a simple wooden bow, she provides the food for her new family.

Susan Pevensie in Narnia is called the "great archer," while her sister Lucy is a "great surgeon" (Lewis 109). Susan admits that she "hated killing things," (121) a phrase that makes her sound squeamish and completely unlike Katniss (though Peeta says almost the same thing). In fact, Susan uses the bow to defend her little sister, a common role for the heroine.

Warrior women frequently liken girlishness to feebleness, as Katniss does. She makes herself an asexual warrior, rejecting Gale's interest and preferring to only be his hunting partner. In fact, she objects to Peeta's declaration of love because, as she claims, it makes her look "weak" (*HG* 135). To Katniss, strength is impenetrable armor without frothy dresses or gentle emotions. All girlish moments, like getting beauty treatments or trying on wedding dresses appall her and "seem to reinforce the idea that Katniss is more powerful when she embraces masculine ways" (Lem and Hassel 124). In Katniss's worldview, one cannot be strong *and* feminine – she must pick one side or the other. Her mother's intricate braid and Madge's pin remain the only tiny feminine tokens she takes to the Capitol.

> A similar archetypal warrior is the moon goddess Artemis. She saves the helpless Iphigenia from sacrifice and defends her own mother with drawn bow, protecting mothers in childbirth and lost children alike. At the same time, she rejects romance, swearing her forest nymphs to chastity and punishing them for the slightest transgression: Bolen notes that she is filled with contradictions. "On the one hand, she rescues women and feminist values from the patriarchy, which devalues or oppresses both. On the other, with her intense focus on goals she can also require that a woman sacrifice and devalue what has traditionally been considered feminine" (71). Her virginity becomes a weapon as she slaughters men in its defense, and punishes her dryads mercilessly for any breech of celibacy. She is the girl dancing with her dryads. She is the independent virgin, uncatchable by man. She is the huntress, famed for tearing the spying Actaeon into shreds with his own hunting dogs. (Frankel, *From Girl to Goddess* 200)

In a similar vein, Tamora Pierce's Alanna disguises herself as the boy "Alan" so she can be a knight. Thus hidden, she becomes the perfect squire to Prince Jonathan with her sword, Lightning. She also ventures into the rough area of town to joke with the King of Thieves, George Cooper. However, a part of her personality remains unexplored. "You fear love," warns the Goddess when she appears to Alanna.

> "You fear Jonathan's love and the love of the Rogue, George Cooper. You even fear the love of Myles, who only wants to be your father. Yet what is there for you to fear? Warmth? Trust? A man's touch?" (Pierce, *Hand of the Goddess* 14).

Indeed, Alanna holds back from all of these. She's spent so long burying her feminine side that she has no idea how to understand it.

Katniss, too, holds back from romance. In the cave with Peeta, she acts romantically by imitating her mother, and even wonders whom Peeta is mimicking. She's so cut off from emotion that she has trouble identifying real love.

After several books, Alanna finds a balance, not with the prince who treats her only as a warrior, but with the joking King of Thieves who calls her Alanna in private so she can nurture her feminine identity. He admires both sides of her, warrior and woman:

> Never before had she been coddled and treated like something precious. Jonathan had always treated her as a comrade, except when they were making love. She usually liked the way the prince handled her, but a small, treacherous part of her longed for the gentle courtesy he gave noble ladies. Now George gave her that courtesy, as well as treating her like a comrade, and she liked the mixture. (Pierce, *Woman who Rides* 180)

Alanna finishes the series with George by balancing her identities as fearless knight and caring woman, invincible in battle and yet eager to have children and pass on these lessons.

Éowyn, in *Lord of the Rings,* suffers from a similar split. She too has cast off much of her feminine side. She's strong and cold, "straight and proud, shapely as a lily, and yet...hard, as if wrought by elf-wrights out of steel" (Tolkien 848). At first, she is most attracted to Aragorn, the best of all warriors. He is courageous and battle-trained, the very tendencies she admires in herself. However, this is not the best start to a relationship. Aragorn has little to offer that Éowyn doesn't already possess: strength, bravery, skill at swordplay. "An Artemis woman may fall in love with a strong man and may then be unable to keep a competitive element out of the relationship, which kills it," notes Jean Shinoda Bolen, author of a book on female archetypes (48).

> This pair makes a perfect team, but tragically often ends in death and parting. The warrior's lover may compete with her and feel jealous of her success. But even if they remain in accord, they are too similar. Neither brings the melding of opposites who join in a perfect relationship as animus and anima [the male and female essences, like yin and yang]. She may regard him fondly, even love him, but he offers her no potential for growth. Each constantly mirrors the other, offering support and acceptance, but no change. (Frankel, *From Girl to Goddess* 208)

Katniss's warrior-partner, of course, is Gale, the one whose forest skills perfectly equal her own. However, as Katniss has learned while surviving the Games and dodging Peacekeepers in District Twelve, Peeta's cleverness may be a better aid for her. More to the point, the warrior woman brings ferocity, strength, and battle skills to the relationship. Thus, her perfect match is not a fellow warrior but someone gentler, a dreamer and magician, a pacifist and savior. This is Peeta, who has all the skills Katniss lacks. He's friendly and funny, always comforting and raising others' spirits "Ironic, encouraging, a little funny, but not at anyone's expense," Katniss muses, in contrast with her own surly personality (*MJ* 299).

When Aragorn, like Éowyn's uncle and brother, refuses to lead her to war, she disguises herself as a man and rides with the company. On the battlefield, she proves herself the bravest, leaping to protect her uncle King Théoden from the monstrous witch-king. Unexpectedly, she feminine side she has always buried proves the only key to his defeat:

> "No living man may hinder me," [the witch-king said.]
>
> "But no living man am I! You look upon a woman. Éowyn I am, Éomund's daughter. You stand between me and my lord and kin. Begone, if you be not deathless! For living or dark undead, I will smite you, if you touch him." (Tolkien 823)

As protector of her helpless uncle, Éowyn destroys the witch-king, though she nearly dies in the attempt. After, she must face her worst fear – all the heroes ride off to battle, leaving her in, as she thinks, "a cage," a place of uselessness where the women of the realm must wait.

In that very House of Healing, Éowyn meets Faramir, Steward of Gondor. If Éowyn represents the perfect body, physical strength and courage, Faramir is more sensitive, an intuitive dreamer and knower. He alone sees her pain and tries to comfort it: "He turned and saw the Lady Éowyn of Rohan; and he was moved with pity, for he saw that she was hurt, and his clear sight perceived her sorrow and unrest" (938). Though she resists him, he speaks with her each day and coaxes her to heal as they wait together for the army to return.

> And Éowyn looked at Faramir long and steadily; and Faramir said: "Do not scorn pity that is the gift of a gentle heart, Éowyn! But I do not offer you my pity. For you are a lady high and valiant and have yourself won renown that shall not be forgotten; and you are a lady beautiful, I deem, beyond even the words of the Elven-tongue to tell. And I love you. Once I pitied your sorrow. But now, were you sorrowless, without fear or any lack, were you the blissful Queen of Gondor, still I would love you. Éowyn, do you not love me?"
>
> Then the heart of Éowyn changed, or else at last she understood it. And suddenly her winter passed, and the sun shone on her.
>
> "I stand in Minas Anor, the Tower of the Sun," she said; "and behold the Shadow has departed! I will be a shieldmaiden no longer, nor vie with the great Riders, nor take joy only in the songs of slaying. I will be

> a healer, and love all things that grow and are not barren." And again she looked at Faramir. "No longer do I desire to be a queen," she said. (943).

Éowyn is no longer devoted to death but to healing, no longer devoted to Aragorn, but to the gentle Faramir, who evokes her protective, intuitive side. Only this supportive partner can heal her wounds, which she has concealed so long beneath her armorlike defensiveness.

Katniss ends her tale on a similar note:

> I know this would have happened anyway. That what I need to survive is not Gale's fire, kindled with rage and hatred. I have plenty of fire myself. What I need is the dandelion in the spring. The bright yellow that means rebirth instead of destruction. (*MJ* 388)

When she settles down, Katniss maintains her atypical gender role, with Peeta to complement her: "Peeta bakes. I hunt" (*MJ* 387). While she fears having children with "a terror that felt as old as life itself," Peeta is the more maternal one, begging for years until he convinces her to have them (*MJ* 388). Together they make two sides of a whole, and together they can become a family.

> Here the non-threatening, gentle lover touches the huntress's heart, where a competitive warrior will fail in this quest...This is the source of the woman's ultimate growth: the sensitive scholar who represents the missing side of the warrior woman's personality. He teaches her compassion, reminding her that "she doesn't need to be so tough all the time." While he supports her goals and willingly submits, he wakens the sensitive side that she lacks. He tempts her towards marriage and motherhood, unlike the fellow warrior, who is happy to remain in a single partnership of equals forever. (Frankel, *From Girl to Goddess* 209)

Katsa in Kristen Cashore's *Graceling* and *Bittterblue* is another young woman divorced from her femininity. Like Katniss, she loathes dresses and plans never to marry. Katsa has a "grace" or magical talent, of warfare, so she can defeat an entire army bare-handed, though she loathes being labeled a killer. Like Katniss in the first book, Katsa obeys the patriarchy in the form of her callous uncle the king. When Prince Po arrives in court, he convinces her that she is stronger than her uncle. Katsa begins to secretly protect the weak and finds herself much happier. Like Peeta, Po is content to let her take charge, commenting, "You may hunt for my food, and pound me every time we fight, and protect me when we're attacked, if you like. I'll thank you for it" (Cashore 181). Despite this modest gesture, his fighting grace appears to match hers perfectly. They reach a turning point, however, when Katsa realizes her mysterious grace is *not* killing but staying alive however she must – through healing, survival skills, and defense.

"But – it's like saying my Grace is life," she blurts.

"And it's not just your own life," Po says, reminding her of the helpless she's chosen to defend (254). Katsa is not a monster as she had feared, but a defender of the helpless. This, too is Katniss's role.

Although she's forced to take part in the games, Katniss is "a hunter but not a killer," her actress Jennifer Lawrence has said. "It's not like she looks around the arena and goes, 'Yeah, I got this.' I think she looks around helplessly and thinks, 'I made a promise to my sister that I would survive; now I have to kill in order to do so.'" ("Let the Games Begin")

Terribly shy and ill-equipped to handle romance, Katsa begins a relationship with Po. As it turns out, his grace isn't warfare either. Though he keeps it a secret, his skill is perception, reading the thoughts of others and understanding them completely in a way defensive Katsa never could. Like Peeta, he teaches his love to connect with people and broadens her sensitivity.

Armed with this new understanding, Katsa rescues young Princess Bitterblue and carries her over impassable icy mountains, sustaining them both with her gift. Bitterblue, like Prim or Rue, represents the childlike feminine side of the heroine. She's sweet, compassionate, and perceptive, and the warrior heroine will defend this inner child at all cost. Katsa slays the tyrant, hurling a dagger to save Bittterblue and protect Po's secret. She ends the story not yet ready to wed Po – like Katniss, she has undergone a harrowing journey and is only on the cusp of discovering who she is once the battle has ended. She returns home, ready to face down her uncle and reclaim her life.

Before she wrote *The Hunger Games*, Suzanne Collins played with unusual gender roles in her *Gregor the Overlander.* Gregor begins the story babysitting his two-year-old sister Boots and doing the laundry. When he falls into the Underland chasing after her, he discovers an underground world of talking rats, bats, mice, and cockroaches. There, he begins questing to save his lost father – even though saving family is the classic heroine's journey rather than the hero's. Though he is the prophesized "warrior," he spends the first book wishing for a sword and never getting one. His solutions are nonviolent, using persuasion and even food: In battle, he sprays the spider queen in the eyes with root beer and taunts Boots with a cookie so she'll torture the spiders with an ear-splitting tantrum.

The young Queen Luxa, by contrast, is the perfect warrior. She performs the coiler, a flying fighting move that "only an extraordinary and flexible rider" can manage (188). When Gregor first sees her, "she executed a perfect double back-flip, twisting around at the last moment to face Gregor's direction, and landed on the ground as lightly as a cat in front of Boots" (25-26). Luxa's and Gregor's traditional gender roles are reversed: Gregor cries when one of their group dies; Luxa reveals that her people think she's "unnatural" since she hasn't cried since her parents' deaths (251). Gregor even teaches Luxa to cook, since she's never done so. Luxa finds herself transferring affections from her cousin, the fellow warrior who's always fought at her side, to Gregor, the most sensitive boy she's ever known.

As the underage queen, Luxa is mentored and supervised by her grandparents. While her grandfather is a great scholar, he's also the more feminized of the pair. He cries in public, and urges idealistic, somewhat naive peace whatever the cost. He is the one to embrace his newly-discovered grandson and welcome him home.

By contrast, Luxa's grandmother, Solovet, is the head of the military and resembles President Coin more than a little. Both authorize secret weapons research and even the murder of children and civilians. Like Coin, Solovet uses solitary confinement and child soldiers to win. It's finally revealed that Solovet imprisoned her own son for a month for disagreeing with her. She drags Gregor's little sisters to the front lines and drafts children to aid in the war effort. By the time it's over, Gregor knows many have lost their innocence.

When Solovet is lost, her lieutenant Perdita is assigned command. Like Commander Paylor in *The Hunger Games*, she is a smart, competent woman leading the military, a quiet reminder that fighting isn't only for men. In both cases, a fair and noble warrior woman takes charge as a counter to Coin/ Solovet, the harsh exploiter of children. As such, she reminds readers that warrior woman can be just or cruel, but are just as strong as men.

Today, the issue of women in combat is hotly debated. Some people protest that women on the front lines can't carry heavy backpacks of supplies or will disrupt the male bonding and camaraderie necessary to morale. Others insist on an end to discrimination. Collins addresses the issue subtly, showing competent leaders like Perdita and Paylor, along with powerful generals Coin and Solovet. No one mocks any of them for being female. Katniss serves alongside male and female troops in *Mockingjay* and is likewise never harassed for her gender.

Collins uses both her series to explore warrior women, and both her heroines fall for the gentle, compassionate boy who challenges them to grow beyond their roles into a fully realized human being. Both must accept adult responsibility and find their way to become leaders, each with the boy who is the dandelion in the spring.

KATNISS LIVES THE ROMAN HISTORIES

In *Mockingjay,* Plutarch Heavensbee explains the Capitol's obsession with "*Panem et Circenses*" (*MJ* 223). If the citizens of Rome had "bread and circuses," food and entertainment, they became spoiled and lazy, willing to let others direct the government. Here is the Capitol, standing as a decadent warning for readers everywhere. It echoes the luxury, splendor and cruelty of Rome, warning us where such heedless extravagance will lead.

The movie takes this imagery to heart. One critic describes the Capitol as having "the dated-futuristic look of a fascist Oz, the lifestyle is somewhere between the late Roman Empire, the court of Louis XVI and the Cirque du Soleil" (Pollitt 10). In the propaganda film introducing the Games, tributes are seen with gladiatorial spears, shields, and brief leather outfits, harkening back to the Roman arena. Katniss's district greets her sacrifice with a three finger salute, started by Christians to represent the trinity as they were executed in the Roman arenas. The triumphal chariot parade down a marble hall like a Roman forum once again sets the scene. Cato and Clove wear bronze scale mail with winged helmets, and the set's hair designer describes Katniss's look as "a helmet out of hair...like a headpiece, almost Gladiator-like" (Laurence). After the Games, Katniss and Peeta are crowned with golden laurel wreaths, the classical symbol for victory.

Rome lived in a world of opulence never seen before or since: After conquering the known world, Caesar celebrated with 22,000 tables of free food and drink at a single banquet. Most famous was the entertainment: exotic animals from Africa, chariot races, and triumphal parades with spectacles of captured treasure and humiliated captive rulers in chains. Some of the gladiatorial combats were immense with entire armies, elephants, and warships.

> Musicians performed between fights. Free meat was served. Figurines of the best gladiators were sold as souvenirs. Indeed, successful gladiators often achieved celebrity status. Their names were known across the Roman Empire. Tales of their heroism were told as bedtime stories to children. (Lewis)

One can easily picture all this happening in Collins's world, where the Games are a year-long spectacle of parades, tours, and propaganda. Even the Vomitorium, a custom of those who could afford overly-rich foods, descends from Rome. Many began to complain about the reckless wastefulness of it all, so Caesar was known to hold an execution or two to keep people in line (Freeman 328-336).

There was also a great deal of corruption: When an attempt to assassinate Emperor Nero went badly, the statesman Seneca was ordered to take the blame and commit suicide, though he hadn't actually been involved (one can see where Seneca Crane got his name). Roman magistrates were shipped off to the provinces as governors, where they abused the people like Peacekeepers, brutalizing and taxing them for profit.

Caesar, like Snow, supported a grain dole for the poor – "a meager wheat or corn ration used for making bread and gruel" (Parenti 209-210). Though it didn't provide for all their needs, it was often the difference between survival and starvation. Romans routinely looked down on the poor – Cicero, repeating the words of his predecessors, called them "city dirt and filth" and "a starving, contemptible rabble" (Parenti 206). They were the Capitol; the districts were beneath their notice.

> Like Katniss and most of the other competitors in the Hunger Games, most gladiators were not given a choice. The majority were slaves or prisoners of war who were forced to fight. There was money to be made in the games, though, and those who managed to live long enough could eventually buy their freedom. (Lewis)

Wealthy first-world readers are meant to be the spoiled Roman audience cheering for gore and blood, not the helpless Tributes condemned to die. Critic Kristin Lewis notes, "Today it seems barbaric – a dark spot in ancient human history. Perhaps what disturbs us most is the image of that thunderous crowd, screaming for carnage, and the question: Would we have screamed right along with them?"

Spartacus the Gladiator, Spartacus the Rebel Leader

"Once the 'Hunger Games' story takes off, I actually would say that the historical figure of Spartacus really becomes more of a model for the arc of the three books, for Katniss," Collins comments (Margolis).

In 73-71 BCE, the gladiator Spartacus escaped slavery and led a revolution across Rome. Born in shepherd-filled Thrace, he was captured and trained in one of Rome's gladiatorial schools. However, he led a revolt of slaves armed with kitchen knives, who escaped into the mountains and hid. As word spread, they quickly gathered thousands of rebels (Freeman 42-43).

Like Katniss, Spartacus grows from someone wanting to survive the arena and earn a comfortable life of celebrity to someone eager to strike out at the spoiled spectators. He, like Katniss, is condemned to fight only for the crime of being born in the districts.

The historian Plutarch describes Spartacus as "a Thracian of Nomadic stock, possessed not only of great courage and strength, but also in sagacity and culture superior to his fortune, and more Hellenic [Greek] than Thracian" (Plutarch, Crassus 8.2). This condescending perspective, that any non-Roman with intellect and courage was overcoming his primitive barbarian origins, was typical of most Roman writings at the time. It's also an attitude shared by Effie Trinket, who speaks condescendingly of district children, faulting them for weak table manners and lack of sophistication.

> Then Clodius the praetor was sent out from Rome against them with three thousand soldiers, and laid siege to them on a hill which had hut one ascent, and that a narrow and difficult one, which Clodius closely watched; everywhere else there were smooth and precipitous cliffs. (Plutarch, Crassus 9.1-9.2)

The *Hunger Games* trilogy displays this type of stand-off more than once. Katniss and her friends are trapped in District Thirteen when the Capitol bombs them, hoping to destroy them in their inaccessible stronghold. Gale employs a similar strategy on the Nut in District Two, allowing them only a single route of escape from their inaccessible fortress. While District Thirteen survives the attack, the Nut's very compactness makes its people vulnerable to explosions within.

> They were also joined by many of the herdsmen and shepherds of the region, sturdy men and swift of foot, some of whom they armed fully, and employed others as scouts and light infantry....Since he could not expect to overcome the Roman power, [Spartacus] began to lead his army toward the Alps, thinking it necessary for them to cross the mountains and go to their respective homes, some to Thrace, and some to Gaul. But his men were now strong in numbers and full of confidence, and would not listen to him, but went ravaging over Italy. (Plutarch, Crassus 9.3-6)

Refugees and runaways pour into District Thirteen as the rebellion grows. Some become soldiers and others, cooks, medics, and other support staff. Through the trilogy, Katniss and Gale fantasize about running off into the forest together and living beneath the Capitol's notice. However, after District Twelve is destroyed, Gale becomes determined to take revenge. He and the firebrands like him ensure that the only outcome is defeat or total victory.

Spartacus defeated the great armies of Rome and won battle after battle. However, he ultimately had no chance. He fell and his rebellion died with him.

Spartacus's doomed quest for freedom from his oppressors has been an image invoked by many revolutionaries who followed. It's also captured hearts worldwide in film and television. In the 1960 film *Spartacus,* the hero is poignant and memorable, reminding viewers that he is not an animal and that the Romans have no right to make him battle and die for their amusement. This is likely the theme Collins is channeling into her own work, along with thoughts on heroism, rebellion, and martyrdom. In the most quoted moment in the film, the Romans demand that the rebels surrender Spartacus. Each person there claims "I am Spartacus" to shield him. Katniss's team all sacrifice themselves in moments echoing this incredible heroism, all so their beloved Mockingjay can survive.

THE DEATH OF CAESAR

The tale of Julius Caesar reaches us from Shakespeare in a version he borrowed heavily from Plutarch. An overwhelming set of parallels appear, especially through the many names transposed into *The Hunger Games*: Caesar and his wife (Cal)Purnia, and rebels Cinna, Portia, Brutus, Flavius, and Messalla. Brutus and Cato are cast as Career Tributes, Mark Antony's wife Octavia becomes a member of the prep team, and *Antony and Cleopatra*'s Enobarbus is remade as the bloodthirsty Enobaria.

Julius Caesar is a story about power and loyalty, as is *The Hunger Games.* Caesar has conquered the world, as Snow has, but both turn tyrannical as they pamper their bored Capitol citizens and oppress the districts. In Snow's actor's (Donald Sutherland's) eyes, Collins's novel is about "the decaying fabric of an empire and the struggle of an oligarchy of the privileged to try and keep that fabric together" ("Letters from the Rose Garden"). Other themes of Shakespeare's play include the discussion of when a revolution is necessary and the fleeting nature of power: The play begins with the comment that the citizens of Rome once cheered Pompey and now cheer Caesar "that comes in triumph over Pompey's blood" (I:i:53). Following the play, Mark Antony, and then Octavian seize power – each time, soldiers die and nothing truly changes. Donald Sutherland adds, "Power perpetuates war and oppression to maintain itself until it finally topples over with the bureaucratic weight of itself and sinks into the pages of history…leaving lessons that need to be learned unlearned" ("Letters from the Rose Garden").

The play opens with the minor character Flavius discovering crowned statues of Caesar. Disgusted, since these are either the public's attempt to nominate Caesar for kingship or Caesar's attempt to make it look like this is happening, Flavius tears them down, crying, "Let no images/ Be hung with Caesar's trophies" (I.i.70-71). This is the first of much political propaganda in the play – another motif *Julius Caesar* shares with *The Hunger Games.*

Though Caesar refuses the crown, publicly, dramatically, it becomes clear that he is determined to rule as a tyrant over the once-balanced Roman Republic. Brutus describes Caesar as an "adder" – a creeping, slithering threat to the people's freedom. While he's still a "serpent's egg" and hasn't claimed the throne, he must die (II.i.14-32). References to President Snow as a snake are frequent, with Snow's "pale, sickly green" skin. Katniss reflects that poison goes well with Snow as it's "the perfect weapon for a snake" (*MJ* 172). Like Snow, President in name and dictator in his acts, Caesar craves absolute power.

This is the reason for his murder, as even Caesar's allies fear he's becoming a tyrant. On the Ides of March, Caesar's trusted allies gather in the Senate. There, the murderers surround Caesar and stab him many times. The setting of their crime is deliberate, making the murder not a cowardly back-alley mugging but a political statement in the sight of the people. Upon seeing that his favored friend Brutus is among the murderers, Caesar gives up struggling, pulls his toga over his face, and dies. Convinced of the rightness of their cause, the murderers drag Caesar's body to the public forum to proclaim their deed. They try to win over the people with cries of "Liberty! Freedom! Tyranny is dead" (III.i.86), and both the rebels and Caesar's supporters make powerful speeches to sway the crowd. Like District Thirteen's propos, the revolution is about political spin as much as freedom.

Katniss slays Coin in public as well, showing the people their true enemy. When Coin proposes the Games, Katniss realizes Coin is a second Snow. She thinks: "All those people I loved, dead, and we are discussing the next Hunger Games in an attempt to avoid wasting life. Nothing has changed. Nothing will ever change now" (*MJ* 378). While it's possible she kills Coin out of revenge, her thoughts are deliberate, careful. Further, Katniss never acts selfishly or vengefully in the story. She refrains from killing Snow in *Mockingjay* and requests immunity for the hateful Enobaria. Katniss's shot at Coin, like her earlier one at Cato, is more likely defensive, ending the threat of the next dictator that no one else has seen. She's showing love for the Capitol's children as she protects the innocent once more.

> Brutus acts for a similar reason. As he proclaims in the forum:
>
> As Caesar loved me, I weep for him; as he was fortunate, I rejoice at
> it; as he was valiant, I honor him; but as he was ambitious,
> I slew him. (III.ii.25-28)

If the people of Rome wish to remain a free republic and not bow to a tyrant king, Caesar must die.

However, Caesar's friend Mark Antony also has a touch of Katniss in him. When Brutus and the other rebels challenge him, Antony vows his loyalty. Similarly, Katniss realizes Coin is suggesting a final Hunger Games as a way of testing her obedience. Antony vows to obey all Brutus's wishes "with all true faith" (III.i.146-150). So too Katniss votes to continue the Games "for

Prim," saying what Coin wants to hear – that Katniss is fooled and thinks Snow has murdered her sister (*MJ* 378). This frees her to fire her final shot at the true threat to Panem.

Antony too gains the rebels' trust, and they invite him to speak, unaware of Antony's true feelings. When Antony addresses the crowd, he gives a famous speech praising Caesar as the greatest of leaders. Making the crowd his weapon, he urges them to slay the conspirators. Antony's words are so convincing that the crowd murders Caesar's killers by nightfall.

One of these conspirators is Lucius Cornelius Cinna, who in history spent his life trying to improve the lives of the "New Citizens" from the countryside. Eventually, he raised an army against Rome and died in the cause. In Shakespeare's play, an angry mob takes revenge for Caesar's death by trying to kill Cinna. Unfortunately, they attack Cinna the Poet, who only has the misfortune to share a name with Lucius Cornelius Cinna. This doesn't stop them:

> Cinna the Poet: I am Cinna the Poet....I am not Cinna the conspirator.
>
> Fourth Citizen: It is no matter, his name's Cinna; pluck but his name out of his heart, and turn him going. (III.iii.29-34)

This theme of guilt by association likewise echoes through *The Hunger Games*, as Johanna proposes hurling Snow's granddaughter into the Games and Snow tortures Peeta's Avoxes and prep team. By series end, tributes and prep teams have almost entirely been killed, for the crime of association.

In Shakespeare, a battle follows, and scores die, emphasizing the senselessness of this revolution. Brutus, defeated, says he thinks it "cowardly and vile" to commit suicide "for fear of what might fall" but at last he kills himself rather than suffer the humiliation of punishment (V.i.112-113). Katniss too tries to kill herself, fearing torture and public execution. Peeta stops her and she lives on, a memorial to the cycles of rebellion.

SETTING THE SCENE: FAMILIAR CHARACTERS FROM ROME

Caesar would be a logical first name for Snow, the dictator who rules the known world from his wealthy Capitol. However, many consider Julius Caesar a brilliant and heroic leader as well as a tyrant. His name evokes nobility, courage, and all that is regal. In fact, the words "Kaiser" and "Czar" derive from his name. Collins may not have wanted to give Snow such shadings of glory. Coriolanus, along with being less known, is a thoroughly despicable figure in Shakespeare and Plutarch. As such, he brings Snow a more fitting first name.

Besides, there is a second dictator in Panem. John Granger, the Hogwarts Professor, references Matthew 22 with its "Render unto Caesar what is

Caesar's" to remind us that biblically, "Caesar" refers to a *coin*, adding:

> In *Mockingjay*, the head of government and power that Katniss must answer to, who tries to kill her and does arrange the death of Prim, and whom Katniss assassinates at story's end is named Coin because she is Caesar, the embodiment of the regime. (Mockingjay Discussion 13)

Coriolanus Snow and Alma Coin are two sides of the same dictator – both are Caesar. Coin and Snow both believe in controlling the population, one through overindulgence and one through scheduling and rules. Coin even has eyes "the color of slush," (*MJ* 10) a type of snow as murky gray as her ethics. This similarity is a reminder, echoing the theme of *Julius Caesar*, that another tyrant always comes to take the empty throne.

The name goes to Caesar Flickerman, a larger-than-life personality. True, he's no dictator, but as emperor of the airwaves and controller of the media, Katniss sees him as the establishment. His name may also hint at actor Sid Caesar, known for the celebrity interview show *Caesar's Hour*. A "Flickerman" is a dramatic documentary about someone's life, a good name for the ultimate interviewer.

His co-host, Claudius Templesmith, was another Roman emperor. He had a particular interest in improving laws and presiding over trials, so his counterpart in Panem rules the ultimate trial, the Games. Emperor Claudius was also known for a great three-day tournament. Called the festival of the Secular Games, it marked the 800th birthday of Rome. The Games are the Capitol's focus and place of worship, their temple in a way, thus the name Templesmith. Oddly, the emperor was also known for giving the provinces equal status with Rome. Perhaps, like Plutarch Heavensbee, this Capitol character has rebel leanings.

> Mestrius Plutarchus (known later as Plutarch) was a priest at the temple of Apollo at Delphi. He became a celebrity in the Roman Empire thanks to his extensive essays and speeches, now known as the *Moralia,* which slyly pointed out the moral deficiencies of those who ruled Rome. The historical Plutarch was interested in moral questions and devoted to preserving free will, much like Katniss's Plutarch. Once famous, Plutarch turned to recording the famous figures of his day. His *Lives* was a famous work of biography, pairing each famous Roman with a similar Greek hero. He wrote on Caesar, Coriolanus, Romulus, Cato, Brutus, and other characters whose names appear in Collins's series. (Frankel, *Katniss* 53)

This biography series was more designed to flatter political figures of his day than record the strict truth. Much of Collins's source material on Rome clearly comes from these biographies and Shakespeare's adaptations of them, making Plutarch a logical storyteller to present the Mockingjay rebellion to the public: He, like Collins, is the transmitter of Katniss's story. Like him, Katniss's Plutarch retells events as propaganda, using them to present an agenda rather than record the literal truth. Both Plutarchs are concerned with answering questions about the nature of morality and free will. His last name, "Heavensbee" comes from "Life of Pericles," one of the chapters in *Plutarch's Lives*: "Diopeithes introduced a bill that those who did not recognize the gods, or who taught theories of the *heavens, be* prosecuted" (Arrow 218).

Cato the Younger according to Plutarch was known for being virtuous and honest, a high principled conservative and Caesar's political enemy. Though from the provinces, Cato was a capitol supporter, urging that candidates for Tribune be required to be significantly wealthy. When Cato lost his war against Julius Caesar, he decided to commit suicide to end his shame. His grotesque, prolonged death scene, recorded in *Plutarch's Lives*, provides insight why the career tribute tortured all night by mutts shares his name:

> Cato drew his sword from its sheath and stabbed himself below the breast. His thrust, however, was somewhat feeble, owing to the inflammation in his hand, arid so he did not at once dispatch himself, but in his death struggle fell from the couch and made a loud noise by overturning a geometrical abacus that stood near. His servants heard the noise and cried out, and his son at once ran in, together with his friends. They saw that he was smeared with blood, and that most of his bowels were protruding, but that he still had his eyes open and was alive; and they were terribly shocked. But the physician went to him and tried to replace his bowels, which remained uninjured, and to sew up the wound. Accordingly, when Cato recovered and became aware of this, he pushed the physician away, tore his bowels with his hands, rent the wound still more, and so died. (*Plutarch's Lives*, Cato the Younger, 70.5-6)

Enobaria is the outsider of the Quarter Quell, a loner without friends or loved ones. She votes to continue the Hunger Games "almost indifferently," suggesting only that the Capitol deserves "a taste of their own medicine" (*MJ* 369). In Shakespeare's *Antony and Cleopatra,* the cynical character Enobarbus offers advice that's equally callous and sarcastic. He watches from the sidelines, not bothering to participate in the war. Meanwhile, Antony and Cleopatra's passionate love lead them to defy Caesar's heir Octavian, rebel against Rome, and finally die in a star-crossed romance, echoing some of Katniss and Peeta's tale.

Enobarbus's historical inspiration, Gnaeus Domitius Ahenobarbus, was Pompey's ally, then Caesar's, then Brutus's, then Mark Antony's, then Octavian's, switching each time to what he hoped was the winning side. In training, Enobaria joins hands with the other tributes, offering a moment of solidarity. However, in the Games, she stabs Beetee and tries to murder the other contestants. When she's captured in *Catching Fire,* Boggs points out that the Capitol will likely let her go, since she's their ally. Nonetheless, Enobaria betrays the Capitol and allies herself with Coin in the end, even wearing the rebel uniform to show that she's chosen the winning side. By doing so, she survives the war.

Collins's more briefly-mentioned characters also derive from Shakespeare's Roman plays. Katniss's film director, Cressida, is almost certainly named after the traitorous heroine in Shakespeare's *Troilus and Cressida.* Known best for betraying her city, the heroine uses clever speeches and well-turned phrases, appropriate for her namesake, a maker of propaganda. Messalla, Cressida's assistant, is another traitor. Historically, he conspired with Brutus, and then left him for Octavian. When Octavian praised him, Messalla commented, "Indeed, O Caesar, I have ever been on the better and juster side" (*Plutarch's Lives,* Brutus, 53.2). Plutarch's assistant, Fulvia, is named for a woman just as fickle. Her second husband switched allegiance from the Roman majority party to the one that favored the common people, much like Panem's Fulvia and her boss, Plutarch. The historical woman went on to wed Mark Antony and raise a rebellion against Rome.

King Darius the Great (who lived about 500 years before Caesar and his friends) never battled the Romans but he did battle their ancestors the Greeks. He was a fair and just lawmaker, much like Darius the Peacekeeper. As such, he remains an anti-Capitol power who, like many Roman rebels, appears in *Plutarch's Lives.* Plutarch also described Alexander the Great's campaign to conquer the kingdoms near the Tigris River – in his histories, the Tigris was where the enemy lived. The woman Tigris, though camouflaged under tiger stripes and helping Katniss and her friends disguise themselves, may be inspired from this source. Plutarch even wrote about the mythical hero twins Castor and Pollux in his essay on brotherly love.

In his *Lives,* he describes the savage Romulus, killer of his twin brother, Remus. Collins may be hinting that it was a crime for Romulus the Peacekeeper to savagely whip Gale in the square as all men are brothers deep down. Plutarch notes, "Theseus, although he had suffered no wrong at their hands himself, sallied out in behalf of others [against King Minos, who demanded a tribute of innocent youths]; while Romulus and Remus, as long as they themselves were not harmed by the tyrant, suffered him to wrong everybody else" (Plutarch, "Comparison of Theseus and Romulus," 1.3). Katniss, as described elsewhere in this book, is the Theseus of Collins's world, who ends the tribute forever. In his comparison to Theseus, Romulus is someone who lets the tyrant prey on others, a good parallel for the brutal Peacekeeper.

The prep team all take their names from rebels and pawns: Flavius is a rebel in *Julius Caesar*, while Octavia (wife of Mark Antony) and Venia (short for Lavinia, a founding mother of Rome) were both helplessly given to powerful men in marriage. In the cells of District Thirteen, Katniss mourns that her prep team have become similar pawns, held hostage for her good behavior. Lavinia the Avox is likewise a victim of the series. She has a more disturbing namesake as the abused Lavinia from *Titus Andronicus*, who has her tongue cut out.

As shown, *Plutarch's Lives* contributed many of Collins's characters including Brutus, Caesar Flickerman, Castor, Cato, Cinna, Claudius Templesmith, Coriolanus Snow, Darius, Enobaria, Flavius, Fulvia, Messalla, Octavia, Pollux, Portia, Purnia, Romulus Thread, Seneca Crane, Tigris, and Venia. Theseus and Spartacus, her inspirations, also have chapters in Plutarch's *Lives*.

Shakespeare's Roman plays offer almost as many characters: Enobaria and Octavia from *Antony and Cleopatra*. Cressida the traitoress from *Troilus and Cressida*. Lavinia, Martin, and Titus from the grisly *Titus Andronicus*. Brutus, Caesar Flickerman, Cato, Cinna, Claudius Templesmith, Flavius, Messalla, Portia, and Purnia from *Julius Caesar*. Of course, one more remains: The evil mastermind of *Coriolanus*.

Coriolanus

Shakespeare's *Coriolanus* is definitive, though once again his version owes many details to Plutarch. Plutarch describes that Coriolanus "had undertaken a fierce and implacable war for the overthrow and destruction of his country, not that he might recover and regain it" (Plutarch, "Comparison of Alcibiades and Coriolanus" 2.5). The parallels with President Coriolanus Snow are clear: He's willing to tear the Capitol to pieces and let his citizens die in booby traps, all to win the war. "To get power by acts of terror, violence, and oppression, is not only a disgrace, it is also an injustice," Plutarch adds (1.4).

Shakespeare's play opens with rioting because Gaius Marcius Coriolanus is withholding grain from the starving citizens. He feels the lower-class farm workers don't deserve food because they're not in the military. Meanwhile, those in his capitol have plenty to eat and care nothing for the farmers. A rebellion begins as the oppressed citizens demand justice.

> First Citizen: You are all resolved rather to die than to famish?
> All: Resolved, resolved.
> First Citizen: First, you know Caius Marcius [Coriolanus] is chief enemy to the people.
> All: We know't, we know't.
> First Citizen: Let us kill him, and we'll have corn at our own price. (I.i.3-8)

This is the story of a revolution: the oppressed country folk against the might of Rome. One military figure warns the starving rabble

> You may as well
> Strike at the heaven with your staves as lift them
> Against the Roman state. (I.i. 59-61)

Rome has too much technology, too numerous armies for the revolution to win. But Coriolanus is a monstrous tyrant who doesn't even value the soldiers wounded in his service. All the same, he flatters and manipulates the politicians so he can be elected consul. Once he has what he wants, he dismisses all those who helped him, as President Snow executes his own favored allies.

Like Snow, Coriolanus is a completely unsympathetic figure. Finally declaring war on his own capitol, he insists he would rather take spiteful revenge on his own citizens than preserve his life. He's executed by the rebels, even as he proclaims he's better than they are.

KATNISS THE HUNGRY: FOOD IN *THE HUNGER GAMES*

You are what you eat" although in Panem this could be stretched to include "what you're named after" and "what you can catch." A "Gale" destroys crops, as does "Snow." A "Coin" can buy and sell food but cannot produce it. But Katniss and Peeta (pita) are both staple foods, capable of feeding people all by themselves. They are the true saviors of Panem.

President Snow eats dove, heartlessly devouring a well-known symbol for peace. The incredibly self-sufficient Finnick is an able fisher. In *Catching Fire,* Katniss and Gale conspire in the woods while roasting chestnuts – these tiny heated kernels represent the slowly heating kernels of their rebellion. Katniss also gives Bonnie and Twill seeds and beans, suggestive of the seeds of revolution Katniss is also offering them.

Hunger is the day-to-day weapon used to torture the citizens of the districts "as a weapon to control populations," as Collins puts it (Blasingame 726). Food also figures heavily in Katniss and Peeta's courtship, smoothed by lamb stew and loaves of bread. Since food is revered in District Twelve, Katniss and Peeta are truly horrified to see the Capitol banquet where the prep team vomits and wastes food. In a series called *The Hunger Games,* Peeta is a baker – feeder of the hungry. Katniss is a hunter. As such, both are saviors of the world, fixers of the districts torn by the wasteful Capitol and the cruelty of hunger.

Bread

Our heroes live in a world named after bread, Panem. Thus bread is the most basic, most important food in the story. In fact, bread from Peeta's bakery appears in chapter one, shared between Gale and Katniss as the first food in the series.

In many religions bread or bread and salt represents a meal. It's a sign of sacred hospitality – when one person offers and another receives, there is peace between them. District Twelve follows this tradition by making bread part of its marriage ceremony, symbolizing a young couple forming a new household for themselves, filled with the food of plenty. Even if the couple can't afford a celebration meal or fine clothes, they have a ceremony with bread toasted over their first fire and sing the traditional song. Bread, fire, song, and home – all the things sacred in Katniss's life.

Peeta, of course, is "the Boy with the Bread" to Katniss. Despite the odd spelling, his name resembles "pita," a humble brown bread nothing like fancy bakery loaves. "The flat dense loaves" of District Twelve might even resemble pita. He comes to be a source of food for her, offering her life as a child and security as an adult. Peeta smells of cinnamon and dill to Katniss, homey baking smells. As such, he's a tiny haven in a troubling world. Literary analyst John Granger sees him as a savior because of the bread imagery:

> "Peeta," the man of town and "Boy with the Bread," has a name that means bread (pita) as well as a vocation as a bread baker. As a child, he gives two loaves of bread to Katniss that he purchases sacrificially (he is beaten for it by his mother), bread which saves her from physical starvation and the eating of which immediately inspires her to think of her "Family Book" and the means to provide for her mother and sister. His bread, in effect, saves her. In a world named "Bread" (Panem is the accusative case form of the Latin word for Bread), I think it is transparent that Peeta or "Peter" is an icon of the Christ, the world creator, Who in St. Peter's church at least, is received as Bread, and Who loves the world and every soul in it sacrificially. (Granger, "Unlocking 'The Hunger Games'")

When Peeta gives Katniss the two loaves, she regards his gift as life itself, a debt she can never repay. Carrying the bread home, she insists that her mother and sister join her at the table properly. She slices the bread nicely and pours tea, reminding them that this is a sacred family moment, not a time to fall on the food like starving animals.

Bread is also heavily symbolic of the districts. The District Eleven crescent roll is shaped like the moon of planting time, dotted with seeds for their agriculture. District Three's square rolls are uniform like technology – unknown to Katniss, they mechanically count down the seconds until their rescue from the Quarter Quell. District Four has a fish-shaped loaf tinted with seaweed. Katniss considers the "ugly drop biscuits" from her own district humble and embarrassing like her district itself (*HG* 98). In the Capitol, Katniss orders puffy bread but it doesn't fill her – like the Capitol citizens, it has nothing of substance to it.

MEALTIME

The series is dominated by meals – The meal of raisin-nut bread and mint tea after Peeta throws her the loaves. The family dinner Katniss prepares for the reaping, which Prim and her mother must eat alone like a funeral banquet.

In the arena, every bite of food is rationed, and outside it, Katniss records the starvation meals of District Twelve, disgusting rations of District Thirteen, luxurious Capitol cuisine. Each meal offers an important glimpse into this world, showing by the foods served who the people of districts, Capitol, or Games are and how they live. Particularly significant meals include the following:

- Katniss's breakfast with Gale, family lunch, and uneaten dinner on Reaping Day
- Peeta's bread
- The roasted pig and the Gamemakers
- Groosling with Rue
- The lamb stew in the cave
- The "Feast" at the Cornucopia
- The Victory Banquet of *Catching Fire*
- The Victors' training meals
- Toasting bread at a District Twelve wedding
- The shellfish feast in the Quarter Quell
- Finnick and Annie's wedding
- Peeta joins Katniss and her friends for beef stew
- The canned food horde in the Capitol
- Tigris's meal
- Katniss begins hunting again

Haymitch seems to drink his meals, but as he and Effie join Peeta and Katniss for Capitol dinners, they are becoming a type of family. In one notable moment in the movie, Haymitch covers his glass, refusing more alcohol as he becomes more serious about training his students. Of course, Katniss sits down to their first meal and nearly stabs his hand, desperate to convince him she's serious about surviving. Despite this rocky start, their meals soon become a place of camaraderie and friendship despite proper Effie's cries for table manners. At one, Octavia sneaks a recovering Katniss a roll, at another, Cinna orders her extra chocolate fondue.

In training for her first Games, Katniss lunches with Peeta. In the second, all the tributes sit together. Katniss's sphere of allies is widening. Likewise, her District Thirteen meals expand from eating with Gale to joining Delly, Annie, Finnick, Johanna, and even a wounded Peeta.

The food in District Thirteen is bland and uniform, reflecting Katniss's hopelessness. Flavorless turnips, scoops of boiled grain, not enough of anything. Every calorie is counted and regulated for optimum performance. Here food is not something to celebrate, only something to aid efficient labor and military training. The rest of life, from housing to weddings, proceed in the same way. After she agrees to work for Coin (selling out in a way),

Katniss writhes at the sliminess of the fish and okra stew. Feeling unbearably trapped by the inflexible system, Katniss wheedles permission to hunt. After, flecks of venison appear in the soup and her mood improves. The beef stew meal becomes a sign of hope, with better food from their first District Eight shipment. It is also a sign of hope for Katniss, as Peeta leaves the hospital to eat it with her.

By contrast, the Capitol serves pheasant and goose liver pate, foods our modern society associates with wealth. There are Roman foods like suckling pig, doves, whole roasted cows and waterfalls of wine. Other foods make it clear the Capitol reflects present-day America: roast beef, chocolate fondue, pumpkin soup. Katniss samples decadent chocolate cake and jellies like jewels. In the movie, all these exotic treats appear in a rainbow of colors, piled in towers of pastries and sweets on the train. This candy store approach bombards Katniss with all she's never been allowed, a final treat before death.

The Gamemakers eat heavily while watching the training. This emphasizes their wealth – they can snack nonstop all day. Katniss shoots their opulent roasted pig with a chilling metal arrow, reminding them this isn't just a dinner party – her underprivileged, undernourished life is at stake. The apple she strikes is a symbol of goddesses and femininity, a blow for the young Artemis against the overweight greedy force of the patriarchy.

District Twelve

The portrayal of District Twelve, its citizens, and its woods offers a great deal of food symbolism. The forest is a place of safety, but also one of abundance and happiness. Katniss and Gale share their first meal of Mellark bread and Prim's goat cheese under a tree. Further, Katniss only smiles when she's there, for her district is a place of repression and cruelty.

The harsh life of District Twelve is emphasized by what they eat: Greasy Sae serves wild dog to people starved for meat, Katniss kills her pet lynx because he frightens off game. At the same time, Katniss shoots with respect, killing animals quickly and painlessly. She shows off her talents by shooting game as tiny as squirrels (through the eye every time!) and as powerful as deer. Both are known for being fast, like Katniss. Squirrels hoard food and deer are excellent runners, always alert and cautious. As such, they take qualities from Katniss herself. Likewise, Prim's goat is a useful, helpful, sweet animal like Prim herself. It gives Prim the power to become a food provider, in a legal, publicly-approved manner, compared with rule-breaking Katniss.

The foods they eat, from Prim's soothing cheese to Katniss's illegal gatherings become a part of who they are. Haymitch, for instance, drinks white liquor. His alcohol lacks the color of Katniss's hopeful dandelions or the evergreens of survival. In fact, it turns him colorless and helpless himself.

To hide her meadow excursion, Katniss buys peppermints for Prim. They're a childish candy and a sharp contrast: once the only thing in the house was mint leaves, and now Katniss can buy fancy sweets on a whim. Their childishness has a similar feel to Katniss's youthful candlelight dress – trying to make her appear young and innocent rather than scheming. They are also artificial, suggesting obedience to the Capitol and its way of life. Of course, her scheme fails, and she and Peeta are sent back to the Games.

Young Katniss and Prim spend their lives gazing through a window at forbidden desserts – there is no sweetness or color to their lives. The window is a clear symbol – they can watch rich people's lives enviously but never taste. In *Catching Fire,* Peeta supplies them with frosted cookies, indicating Katniss's new wealth but also Peeta's love. Even rich as he is, he remains a nurturer and baker, just as wild Katniss continues to hunt – food is tied up in who they are.

"Katniss" of course is a kind of cattail root, as she tells us in the first few pages. Calling her a staple food grounds her firmly in the real life responsibilities of survival. One critic notes, "It's a practical name: no frills, no fuss, all about the bottom line. Survival" (Barnes 21). A katniss root is as nourishing as a potato, a quality vital to Katniss, provider of food for her family. Elizabeth Baird Hardy adds: "It is known as duck-potato, appropriate for someone whose sister always has a duck tail…but also as swan potato, wapatoo, tule potato, and, most commonly, as arrowhead." Indeed, it's the most "arrowlike" of plants, a good representation for Katniss the archer.

Taking her name from a meadow plant links Katniss forever with the wilds outside District Twelve. "As long as you can find yourself, you'll never starve," her father teases (*HG* 52).

> While this is literally true, Katniss survives by keeping herself grounded – remembering who she is and what she cares for. Indeed, if she can find herself under so many costumes and identities like the Mockingjay, she will survive. Though the Capitol trains its Tributes in brutality, encouraging them to turn on each other, Katniss follows her instinctive compassion and bonds with Rue and Peeta in the Games. This saves her in the end. (Frankel, *Katniss* 13)

Under the sparkling gowns and artificiality of the Capitol, Katniss keeps the "genuineness" that makes the Capitol love her.

"Everdeen" is two letters off from "evergreen," which is fitting beside the "Hawthornes" and other plant names from the outer districts. Evergreens, like the katniss, are edible, for Katniss and her allies drink pine needle tea in the series. Pines and other evergreens thrive in areas of low nutrition – that's why they don't shed leaves. Instead, they remain sharp and strong like Katniss herself. Further, their eternally green look is a symbol of new birth and reincarnation – in the depths of winter they promise a new springtime to come. Green is a color of life and growth, like the dandelion greens and mint tea Katniss serves her family. It's her favorite color, an image of her forests that she keeps in her heart.

Just important as these plants to Katniss is, as she says, "the dandelion that reminded me that I was not doomed," the tiny yellow flower she sees blooming in the school yard (*HG* 32). Even in the sterile, unhappy town of District Twelve, a few small flowers grow. Inspired by its tiny light, Katniss finds her courage and begins foraging in the woods. Like the pine, the dandelion is sharp-toothed and spiky, a tough survivalist and useful food.

"Rue is a small yellow flower that grows in the meadow" (*HG* 99) beside the dandelions that remind Katniss of hope and survival. The rue plant also thrives in areas of low nutrition and is used as a bitter seasoning. Its taste created the verb "to rue" – to regret or wish something hadn't happen. Whenever Katniss pictures Rue, she regrets the waste of her short life.

> Katniss always pictures Rue with her arms spread, ready to take flight, a figure of freedom in a world of tyranny. The rue plant's older Roman name *Ruta* is from the Greek *reuo* (to set free), because this herb cures some diseases and poisons, as Rue herself cures Katniss's tracker jacker stings. It was later called Herb-of-Grace because people sprinkled holy water in churches with brushes of rue. Rue's short life becomes a blessing and grace for Katniss, protection in the Game and then a memory of beauty and sweetness through the rebellion. (Frankel, *Katniss* 58)

Primroses have edible parts, but they are better known for their medicinal uses. Prim, of course, plans to become a doctor in District Thirteen. Katniss sees her sister as a delicate, pretty flower in need of protection.

> Like Prim herself, the plant is cheerful, lovely, and bright, often thriving in areas other plants don't want. It will grow nearly everywhere, turning even ugly little patches of fairly useless dirt into gardens. Prim, too, thrives in an ugly, destructive environment, bringing beauty and light wherever she goes. And, like Prim, who makes herself at home in District 13, or anywhere else she goes, primroses can adapt and grow in nearly any environment, although, interestingly, they are not common west of the Rockies (the region of the Capitol, where Prim herself dies). (Hardy)

Snow, of course, is the enemy of those who forage for food and gather lifesaving plants. As Katniss gathers the forest's natural bounty, Snow rules a world of order and artificiality. His hybrid hothouse roses are "lush pink, sunset orange, and even pale blue" (*MJ* 354). To Katniss, they're like plant mutts, unnatural and changed. She describes entering the garden at last but "not touching, because I have learned the hard way how deadly these beauties can be" (*MJ* 355). The greenhouse is a place of man's power over nature, taming the environment and reshaping it for pleasure. Snow's garden, like his dungeons, represents a place where flowers and flowerlike children are imprisoned and changed to suit his purposes.

The white rose Katniss plucks there is a symbol of her own lost innocence, along with the innocence of Peeta, Rue, Prim, and all the others that have been lost. A white rose also represents martyrdom. By insisting he wear the rose to his death, she is blaming Snow for all the tragedy. It's no wonder Coin is happy to pin it on him, literally and figuratively. This echoes a moment out of Shakespeare in which mad Ophelia hands the tyrant king flowers, particularly the rue flower of regret, before committing suicide. The king's schemes have killed her own father as well as countless others.

> While Claudius must bear regret for murder, Ophelia bears it for her losses – for those loved ones like her father who have died in this struggle for political ambition. Katniss echoes this moment when she gives Snow a white rose, the artificial Capitol flower that has always in her mind been linked with blood and death. Ophelia and Katniss both willingly go to their deaths but take a final moment to give the tyrant this particular gift, showing they know about the deaths that stain him forever. (Frankel, *Katniss* 58)

Snow's roses provide no nourishment, but only serve to conceal the blood-drenched scent of his breath. In fact, roses represent blood in folklore because of their deep red color. Collins is haunted by this image, as she described her father taking her to the beautiful crimson poppy fields of Flanders, a scene that seemed "straight out of *The Wizard of Oz*" – until her father recited a war poem. "O.K., so this moment becomes transformative, because now I'm looking out onto that field and wondering if it was a graveyard," she explains (Dominus). This moment echoes Katniss's at the end, as she gazes at her children in their lovely meadow and remembers the dark truth beneath it.

In the Games

A cornucopia is a sign of endless food given by the gods, a creepy classical symbol for the Gamemakers to toss in (though consistent with their Greek/Roman feel). In this symbolism, the Gamemakers are the gods who hurl down firestorms or summon night on a whim. Their "feasts," however, encourage the tributes to kill and die for the precious supplies. Of course, these supplies always go to the favored and powerful Careers, leaving Katniss and Rue to pick at the leftover scraps around the edges. This becomes a perfect reflection of their lives in the districts. A Cornucopia was a goddess symbol, like the forest (Walker 90). In the Games, both are polluted and changed: the Cornucopia brings death, like the Capitol's mutts. In the Quarter Quell, Katniss and her friends capture the Cornucopia, only to find its promise of abundance is a lie – this time it holds only death – weapons – rather than life-giving supplies.

Despite trainer Atala's warning, none of the tributes starve in the movie – all are killed. It's difficult to show the prolonged suffering of starvation in a short movie – this would also be why Katniss's dehydration is cut. In the book, however, Katniss is terribly malnourished. Even her amazing hunting powers become useless when the Gamemakers send rainstorms and fire, meant to keep Katniss a helpless pawn.

When possible, she hunts capably, shooting groosling birds and snaring rabbits. In fact, the book turns into a survival guide of sorts, as Katniss gathers cress and heats soup with warm rocks. Collins reports that she "read a big stack of wilderness survival guidebooks" to write the series. As she adds:

> Some things I knew from listening to my dad talking about his childhood. He grew up during the Depression. For his family, hunting was not a sport but a way to put meat on the table. He also knew a certain amount about edible plants. He'd go into the woods and gather all these wild mushrooms and bring them home and sauté them. My mom wouldn't let any of us go near them! But he'd eat them up and they never harmed him, so I guess he knew which ones were safe, because wild mushrooms can be very deadly. ("Conversation")

Indeed, Katniss warns readers never to cat mushrooms if they're not certain and shows the dangers of poisonous berries. Tips on climbing trees and hiding footprints fill the series, offering a new world of knowledge for readers.

Rue gathers roots, nuts, and berries, all tiny simple things concealed in the forest, much like Rue herself. She has the plant knowledge Katniss cannot quite recall, gathering leaves to fix Katniss's tracker jacker stings. Peeta assembles breakfast and gathers berries, though the latter reveals how honestly clueless he is in the woods. Meanwhile, his bakery skills save his life as he paints himself into perfect camouflage. "If only you could frost someone to death," Katniss criticizes, but his talent is meant to nurture, not kill (*HG* 96). To her surprise, she learns that Peeta only gets to eat the stale pieces from the bakery – she is not as well-off and spoiled as she had thought.

The Careers really are that spoiled, as Katniss discovers when she finds one boy carries only a packet of dried fruit. He and his friends have no concept how to survive in the wild, forage, hoard food, or go hungry – all skills Katniss can use to beat them. Though they have always held the advantage, Katniss's lifelong starvation and want has made her resourceful and clever. Food becomes her weapon and tool: Katniss destroys the Careers' supplies by shooting at a bag of humble apples. She tosses nuts to find the force fields in the Quarter Quell. Most importantly, after the nightlock berries have killed

Foxface, Katniss uses them to defy the Capitol and threaten suicide.

Similarly, Haymitch signals Katniss with food. One pot of broth equals a kiss. Being romantic with Peeta brings them a dinner for two. Katniss must drug him with sleep syrup. Of course, District Eleven's crescent roll, meant to show their thanks and support, is the most heartbreaking sponsor gift.

In the Quarter Quell, the mentors send bread to almost every meal. As well as a code, it's a symbol of encouragement: You get more food if you work together. The shellfish bake on the beach in the Quarter Quell represents a moment of social bonding between the uncertain allies. They are not starving trainees but experienced survivalists, so much that they have plenty to eat and can even afford to kill all the remaining shellfish to escape. Their sponsors send a tasty sauce, meant to hearten them in their solidarity. At the same time, its spiciness and red color may foreshadow the building tension and the fiery explosions to come.

Food appears constantly through the series as Katniss documents every meal. In the Games and at home, she is starving, parceling out each piece of groosling or basket of dandelion greens because it's all she has. In the Capitol, she is overwhelmed and sometimes disgusted with the wasteful abundance. The constant obsession with food emphasizes how central it is to Katniss, the one person who keeps her family from starving while always on the brink of hunger herself. Even after she becomes rich, she remains constantly aware of the underprivileged, "the emaciated bodies of the children on our kitchen table as my mother prescribes what the parents can't give. More food" (*CF* 80). Through Katniss, Collins reminds us of people today who think like this, constantly considering their next meal because they can barely afford to eat.

KATNISS AND BELLA
THE LOVE TRIANGLE AND MODERN TEENS' FANTASY MEN

It's not surprising that everyone is comparing *Twilight* and *The Hunger Games*. Both first person books are the hottest in the young adult section, and that's only the beginning. As literary critic Sarah Seltzer notes in "Hunger Pangs: Hunting for the Perfect Heroine":

> Both have a teenage female narrator who catapults readers through her story at a breathless pace, with an occasional twist of wry humor. Both of those narrators are embroiled in a love triangle, each caught between two young male suitors; and in both, the accompanying canoodling stays firmly at first base until the final book in the series. Both heroines get bruised, burned, and threatened, and must be rescued by (and rescue) their love interests at regular intervals.

The major difference between the heroines is that Bella is caught in a gothic love story, while Katniss is a warrior leading a rebellion against a dystopian dictator. While their love triangles are similar, the characters are wildly different, as are their roles in the plot. And yes, while *The Hunger Games* does contain a love triangle "that's not really what it's about," insists Elizabeth Banks, who plays Effie Trinket in the film. "There's no schoolgirl crush happening here. The stakes are too high for that. This isn't about a first kiss. This is life and death" ("Let the Games Begin").

Katniss herself comments, "The very notion that I'm devoting any thought to who I want presented as my lover, given our current circumstances, is demeaning" (*MJ* 34). As the author of the essay "Team Katniss" protests, "If this were a book about a boy who takes his brother's place at that first reaping, I wonder if we would all be sitting around talking about who he should be with, rather than who we think he should be" (Barnes 19). When Haymitch sarcastically boils her problems down to "boy trouble," Katniss is deeply hurt and flees the room. She and Bella are both protagonists, but the series aren't both romances.

At the same time, when one compares only the love triangles, a cascade of similarities present themselves. The heroines, both considering themselves gawky and unlovable, have two boys competing for them. One is wealthy, pale, high-class, and set apart. He's a pacifist and model of restraint. The other is "the boy next door," darker-skinned, happiest in the outdoors or working with his hands. This one is more hot-tempered, even violent as he trains in combat. Family pressure guides her toward this one, a childhood and family friend. After some struggle, the heroine chooses the first. Why do both heroines choose the same way? What does this reveal about today's young women and their fantasies?

Katniss's name actually originates in her love triangle. Suzanne Collins notes that "Katniss Everdeen owes her last name to Bathsheba Everdene, the lead character in *Far from the Madding Crowd*. The two are very different, but both struggle with knowing their hearts" (Jordan). In Thomas Hardy's classic, Bathsheba Everdene struggles to choose between a dashing soldier and a poor shepherd. Bathsheba, like Katniss, hesitates between these men, one gentle and chaste (Peeta comments that he's never cared for a girl besides Katniss) and one led by his anger. After betrayal and abandonment by the more violent man, Bathsheba, like Katniss, finally weds the quieter suitor.

Love triangles themselves are a popular fantasy. Relationship expert Gilda Carle explains:

> We want to be fought over. It makes us feel more like a prize. And a suitor wants to fight over us, so he feels he has won a prize, something not so easily gotten. In real life, triangles are horrible. But by vicariously enjoying them in books and movies, we can deal with them more appropriately. (Wloszczyna 1)

The Pacifist Protector

Bella's triangle offers the icy-skinned and aloof Edward, who knows a relationship with Bella could destroy her. "His barely restrained passion, the result of the war between his utter devotion to one woman and his animalistic desire to consume her, is reined in by his moral conscience and colored by the mystery of his aloofness" (Cochran 7). As he confides:

> You are so soft, so fragile. I have to mind my actions every moment that we're together so that I don't hurt you. I could kill you quite easily, Bella, simply by accident…I can never, never afford to lose any kind of control when I'm with you. (Meyer, *Twilight* 310)

Though the possibility of killing her is ominous, the rest is comforting – Bella need not be the shy virgin, protesting and putting him off, as Edward himself is slowing their relationship.

Edward may be a vampire, but there has also been significant work done to effectively neuter him as a threat. He calls himself a vegetarian vampire, refusing to prey on people, and he runs from Bella rather than allow himself to be tempted to hurt her. Bella is the one to initiate the first kiss, insisting that they wed and that he make her a vampire so they can spend eternity together. In a story in which the relationship *is* the story, she gets to make all the choices. Edward in turn allows this, arguing only when he fears she's putting herself at risk. When she tries to deepen their first kiss, he stops her "with irresistible force" (*Twilight* 282). Incredible vampire strength, yes, but strength only used to protect the heroine, even from her own lust. Bella need not fear her own passions, as Edward has vowed to protect them both from temptation. Bella notes, "He started to pull away – that was his automatic response whenever he decided things had gone too far" (*Breaking Dawn* 25). Edward laughs in *Eclipse* that "everything is backward" since he and Bella should be arguing opposite sides in the traditional chastity debate (451). Thus, Bella feels empowered by getting to press her needs, while remaining physically and emotionally safe.

When Bella's father Charlie voices concerns about sex, Bella responds, "Edward is very old-fashioned. You have nothing to worry about" (*Eclipse* 59). Critic Kate Cochran identifies Edward as such a consummate Victorian that he's "a secular saint" with his "self-denial and determination to protect Bella, particularly from himself" (12). Chilly Edward's always described as turning to stone, with "marble lips" (*Twilight* 282) and "icy" skin (*Twilight* 283). "I just wanted to write for myself, a fantasy. And that's what Edward is," Meyer explains (Elgin 63). But her fantasy seems shared by millions of American women.

Edward keeps their relationship perfectly chaste, even after their marriage, save for a single encounter, which frightens him. Bella plays the seductress, encouraging Edward, but once more, he insists on a loving but physically cautious relationship. Stephen King explains:

> In the case of Stephanie Meyer, it's very clear that she's writing to a whole generation of girls and opening up a safe kind of joining of love and sex in these books. It's exciting and it's thrilling and it's not particularly threatening because they're not overtly sexual. A lot of the physical side of it is conveyed in things like the vampire will touch her forearm or run a hand over skin, and she just flushes all hot and cold. And for girls, that's a shorthand for all the feelings that they're not ready to deal with yet." ("Exclusive: Stephen King")

An all-too-capable prince is part of the fantasy, at least in *Twilight*. Like Katniss, Bella is a surrogate parent to her entire family and welcomes having someone to take the endless responsibilities off her hands and provide her with wealth, security, and emotional comfort. Edward takes it to the point of eerie stalking, if not outright abuse. He asks Alice to kidnap Bella for the weekend, leaves her for her own good, and threatens to be "overbearingly protective" when other vampires visit (*Twilight* 328). However, the aggressive, controlling figure is part of the infantilizing fantasy – total care and protection.

Though Katniss is a capable warrior, she's reminded that she wouldn't be alive at all without Peeta, her childhood savior. When she is at her most helpless, only eleven, parentless, and huddled starving on the street, Peeta gives her not only bread but hope: "To this day, I can never shake the connection between this boy, Peeta Mellark, and the bread that gave me hope, and the dandelion that reminded me that I was not doomed" (*HG* 32). He also saves her from the Careers in the Games, leaving her angry and frustrated, yet grudgingly admitting that he was there when she needed him.

At the same time, Peeta is completely nonthreatening, admitting willingly that Katniss could easily beat him. Training for the Games, Katniss describes Peeta's incredible strength, tempered by his incredible pacifism. Though he says he'll kill to preserve his own life, Peeta spends the Games first talking and posturing to gain the Career Tributes' trust, and then camouflaged in the river as he submissively waits to bleed to death. Without Katniss, he would not be in contention to win the brutal Games. In the cave, later, he is near death, nobly determined to sacrifice himself rather than let her risk her life at the Cornucopia.

Of course, as a vampire, Edward could easily kill Bella, and he constantly warns her to be afraid of him. Why does this make him an alluring mate? In fact, relationships are scary, and the emotional danger he poses has been transposed to physical danger, a less threatening realm for the main character.

> "I was wishing that I wasn't afraid."
>
> "I don't want you to be afraid." His voice was just a soft murmur. I heard what he couldn't truthfully say, that I didn't need to be afraid, that there was nothing to fear.
>
> "Well, that's not exactly the fear I meant, though that's certainly something to think about." (*Twilight* 262)

In fact, Bella is unfrightened by Edward's description of himself as predator and instead fears risking her heart. She only becomes "more frightened of him than I had ever been" when he drops his stony façade and lashes out at her emotionally. At that moment, she sees the turbulence he's been hiding and "he'd never been less human…or more beautiful" (*Twilight* 264). On one level this is the tale of a vampire in love with his natural prey, but the metaphor is about Bella's readiness to succumb to the dangerous love that will devour her utterly and leave her transformed.

Of course Bella also has disturbing suicidal tendencies, muddying the water further on whether she or Edward is the greater threat to herself. When informed how much Edward wants to literally eat her, she responds with a melancholic, "What are you asking? My permission?...I mean, is there no hope, then?" (*Twilight* 269). "I would rather die than stay away from you,"

Bella tells Edward (*Twilight* 274). These words, usually mere exaggeration, can here be taken as literal truth in this exaggerated tale of a teenage girl who not only vows to die for her love but honestly means it.

After Peeta is hijacked, he, like Edward, longs with every fiber of his being to kill the heroine, with only a thin veneer of shaky rationality preventing it. In fact, Peeta is chained up to prevent this, with an entire district determined to protect Katniss from the threat. Again, the pacifist male reveals his dangerous side, and again, the heroine is more frightened of the emotional pain than the physical pain that reflects it. "It was less painful being strangled," Katniss reveals (*MJ* 191). Though Peeta becomes a soldier, Commander Boggs disarms him immediately. Peeta is no kind of warrior at all in fact; when in danger, his response is to offer suicide to protect the team, not to go out battling. Like Edward, he would rather die himself than hurt his love, creating a distraught, suffering hero, repressed to the point of literal suicide (which Edward attempts in *New Moon*). He's irresistible.

The Rebellious Rival

"The hot-blooded, emotional, impulsive, and russet-skinned Jacob" has tempestuous emotions that echo his werewolf state (Leggatt and Burnett 43). His temper causes him to change, unlike Edward's vampire abilities, which are all about self-denial and control. Jacob provokes similar feelings in Bella. She motorcycles and behaves recklessly with Jacob, but Edward is the voice of caution within her, counseling her not to risk her life. Contrasting Edward's constant restraint, "Jacob twice forces himself on Bella, first through his physical strength, and then through trickery" (Leggatt and Burnett 36).

Gale, like Jacob, is Katniss's partner for dangerous work, sneaking out to the forest each day and breaking the law to forage for their families. Peeta waits inside, following the laws. In the Capitol, Gale's a skilled partner for Katniss, with more discipline and training than she herself has. However, as he develops, Gale becomes a solider and a killer. Worse yet, he advocates dirty tricks in war, bombing the wounded and the medics who care for them. As his actor, Liam Hemsworth, explains:

> Gale is a good, strong-minded person who hates nothing more than he hates the Capitol. He hates everything they stand for. He hates what they do to people. And he doesn't want to give in to what they stand for. I think he gets really frustrated at times and he's constantly trying to think of ways he can get away. (Egan 29)

He uses violence until it turns on Katniss and destroys the one she loves most.

Despite this, Katniss seriously considers Gale as a life partner, keeping readers guessing until the last few chapters. Jacob, however, is less an ideal love for the heroine and more of an obstacle, keeping her from committing to Edward with his competitiveness.

> The character initially existed in the first book as a device to explain the tense relationship between his Quileute tribe and the Cullen clan to Bella, a newcomer to Forks, Wash. He grew into a central character, however, in *New Moon*, and Meyer even went back and put more of him and his father in *Twilight* while it was in the editing stage. (Wloszczyna 2)

He is not a serious contender. "Jacob was never going to be the prince in her story. He is not white, unnaturally beautiful, or wealthy. He cannot, by virtue of his race, species as a shapeshifter/wolf, and socioeconomic position, help her to rise" (Buttsworth 59). He also cannot grant Bella a supernatural existence as Edward can.

While Gale is "the boy next door," very much in Katniss's own class and sphere, Peeta is Other, the higher-class, well-fed doughy boy who used his wealth to save a starving Katniss, much as Edward saved Bella from a bus. Peeta's family is upper-class, like the Mayor's and the other town citizens. Edward's father is the respected town doctor, while Jacob and Gale live on the outskirts of town, close to the forest. They, like their fathers, do manual labor and have only the required education.

Bella's father Charlie is not much wealthier than the Quileutes. He can only afford an ancient truck for Bella, in contrast with the Cullens' many sportscars. Alice brings her expensive dresses since Bella hardly has a closet of them herself. Edward is the pathway to a better life in true Prince Charming fashion; Jacob is not. Bella cooks and cleans and cares for her father's house like so many old-fashioned fairytale heroines, before getting raised up to a Cullen woman and living a princesslike life of luxury and endless wealth. Granted, Rosalie has mechanical skills and Edward encourages Bella to attend college.

> But technical skill is not required of these radiant women and is indulged because they will never need to use it as a profession, unlike Jacob, whose class and ethnic background in these depictions seem to necessitate knowledge of a "trade" rather than aspiration to a profession (Buttsworth 64)

Jacob tells Bella, "I was the natural path your life would have taken…If the world was the way it was supposed to be, if there were no monsters and no magic" (*Eclipse* 599). Indeed, he is Bella's age, while mysteriously old-fashioned Edward would have lived a full century earlier. Jacob is the boy next door, the family friend with little mystery or magic to him. Like Peeta, Edward is everything the other boy's not, and the heroine's path to evolution.

DEEPER WISDOM

Katniss, as a warrior, might logically choose a contrasting partner and discover the gentle baker is her true love. Likewise, the story gives her a significant reason not to pick Gale, as she blames him for what happens to Prim. However, Katniss also finds her loyalty shifting from blustering, angry Gale to the gentle Peeta, who lifts people's spirits with humor and charm. This may indicate a path away from the crude, physical world of the forest toward a higher spiritual realm. Peeta is a painter, Edward a musician. Both spend time with their girlfriends in the indoor world of civilization and higher thought rather than out in the wilderness. In fact, rather than gloomy, mysterious trees, both are associated with a meadow filled with sunlight. This is quite literally an image of peace and enlightenment.

John Granger, like many literary critics, notes the similarities between Bella's and Katniss's boyfriends:

> One of these guys is other-worldly handsome, intelligent, sensitive, artistic, sacrificial, and devoted. And chaste! The guy is a virgin and has never loved anyone the way he loves our heroine. He's given to phrases like "always" and "forever" in statements of his love.
>
> The other guy is a *mensch*, the out-doorsy type. No rocket scientist or saint, he can be a bore sometimes and say off-the-wall unkind things but you know he has your back in a fight and he lives for family and community. ("Mockingjay Discussion 19")

Granger adds:

> – Gale is the body and the passions; he equates with the World and "how men think;"
> – Katniss is the seeking heart, the animating life-force or soul;
> – Peeta is the Divine Mind or spiritual reality; he equates with the Word and "how God thinks."
> Together they are a triptych of the human person – body, soul, and spirit. ("Mockingjay Discussion 19")

This pattern echoes through much of fiction, from Kirk, Spock, and McCoy on *Star Trek* to Harry, Ron, and Hermione. As Katniss and Bella grow from physical creatures to spiritual ones, they cling to the boyfriend who has a deeper perspective to offer. Everyone's favorite moment in *Eclipse* came when a near-sleeping Bella listened to her two guys having a heart-to-heart conversation. Katniss experienced the same on her invasion of the Capitol. This is a moment of peace and camaraderie, with body and mind bonding and making their peace in the lull before a great battle.

Another trend appears in this classic love triangle. Jacob is Native American, while Gale resembles olive-skinned Katniss so closely most people think they're related. Peeta and Edward are light-skinned (dead white in Edward's case). This may be a racial metaphor, or, more likely, an image of the paleness of aristocracy, privilege, and civilization deeply rooted in America's European ancestry as desirable. For the wealthy, pale prince to choose the less-privileged commoner echoes Cinderella, an enticing fairytale for women that cuts deep into our childhood fantasies.

The metaphor hasn't always swung this way. In *Like Water for Chocolate*, Tita chooses the passionate Spanish boy next door over the wealthy European doctor who offers to rescue her from her cruel family. Jane Eyre chooses dark, brooding, savage Rochester, not her well-mannered cousin. And who could forget Cathy's passion for swarthy Heathcliff over repressed Linton?

In the days of Victorian repression and before, women confined to their homes dreamed of the smoldering gothic hero, dark and melancholy, who would tear them from their dull, safe princes. He might be the mysterious sheik, the evil vampire, the dark foreigner. Today, however, teens see too much brutality. The savage, all around us in our lives and on the news, has lost his savor. Girls are retreating to the safer Cinderella fantasy of their childhood. Fairytale adaptations are overwhelmingly popular right now, with a resurgence in young adult novelizations, movies, and television shows.

These modern Cinderellas are frequently assertive women who can take care of themselves: one Cinderella pulls a glass sword from her mother's tree, another tries to win the prince's eye so he can grant her a boon of revenge. Many of these heroines have traditionally male professions, from mechanic to scholar. Still, the fantasy of the sophisticated, sheltered prince loving her for being outspoken and unique predominates the fantasy. If there is a beast present, Beauty prefers the prince.

Katniss, of course, considers the public's interest in her love life "demeaning" and rejects the sparkling gowns she's forced to wear onscreen. By contrast, Sara Buttsworth, author of "Cinderbella: Twilight, Fairy Tales, and the Twenty-First Century American Dream" sees parallels between Bella and many fairytales (beginning, of course, with her name): There's mention of Snow White, Cinderella, Beauty and the Beast, and Little Red Riding Hood. Jacob mutters "Bibbidi-Bobbidi-Boo" when speaking to Carlisle, the fairy godmother of the story (*Breaking Dawn* 237). Bella thinks of Rosalie as a Sleeping Beauty (*Breaking Dawn* 253) and describes Esme, the perfect housekeeper as "like meeting Snow White in the flesh" (*Twilight* 282). But most of all, Bella follows the American Dream that has melded with the Cinderella story: wealth and happiness through self-sacrifice and marriage to Prince Charming. Buttsworth notes, "'Forget Princess, I want to be a Vampire' sums up an entire culture whose ideal of having it all conflicts with the realities of income differences and sexual inequality that still characterize American society" (67).

Similar Stories

Several recent young adult fairytale retellings echo this fantasy, complete with love triangle. Kiera Cass's *The Selection* (2012) recreates Cinderella in a dystopian future. The prince chooses young ladies from their pictures, and, in a reality show much like *The Bachelor,* they compete to charm him. Among these young women, America Singer alone yells at the prince and rejects him. He's captivated. Since she's from the lower class, America persuades the prince to provide food for the starving and improve his world outside the sheltered palace. Soon, her impetuous childhood sweetheart becomes a soldier in the palace and demands her love. By the cliffhanger end of book one, she's failed to resolve her conflict, saying only, "I'm not choosing him *or* you. I'm choosing me" (323). However, as this is Cinderella, it's fairly certain she'll end her tale with the prince.

Snow White and the Huntsman (2012) sees the Huntsman and Duke's son both connecting with the heroine. Again, one is a wild, unlettered son of the forest, the other sculpted and sophisticated. As with *The Selection,* the heroine does not choose, instead, ascending the throne alone as conqueror of her kingdom. Snow White's one romantic scene is with the duke's son…in fact, he is the queen in disguise complete with poisoned apple. The motif of devoted prince as murderer returns, and Snow White sinks to the ground. In this version, however, the Huntsman is the one to kiss her awake and share a soulful look with her at the movie's end. If Snow White does wed the prince, one assumes she'll keep the Huntsman close in her heart.

Summer 2013 many teens are anticipating the first *Mortal Instruments* film. In Cassandra Clare's series, Brooklyn-dwelling Clary Fray is thrust into a world of monsters when she sees a teen kill a demon. This boy, Jace Wayland, seeks her out and tells her she must return home with him and train her magical abilities. He's arrogant and mouthy, an admitted killer who threatens to kidnap her if she won't cooperate. At the same time, he's devastatingly handsome with old-world charm. As Clary is drawn into the realm of magic, she's torn between Jace and her entirely human best friend, Simon. Clary regards Simon as the good boy and Jace as the alluring bad one:

> [Simon] looked like the sort of boy who'd come over to your house to pick you up for a date and be polite to your parents and nice to your pets. Jace, on the other hand, looked like the sort of boy who'd come over to your house and burn it down for kicks (213).

Further, she dreams of dancing with both of them at a ball: Simon is dressed in black, with "dark hair" and "lightly browned skin" while Jace is in white "and his hair and eyes looked more gold than ever" (161). The pale and dark coloring theme repeats here, with Jace highlighted in gold like a prince. Though they have many trials to face before they can live happily ever after,

Jace is Clary's first choice.

Tiger's Curse by Colleen Houck and its sequels (2010-2012) echo *Twilight* in many ways, while also incorporating world myth. Kelsey Hayes, a frustrated foster teen, feels a mysterious bond with a circus tiger. As she soon discovers, he's an enchanted prince from India, forced to take a tiger's shape most of the day. His assistant, Mr. Kadam, whisks Kelsey to India, where she quests with Prince Ren to break the curse and restore him to his human shape. Despite Indiana-Jones-style traps and dangers, the love arc takes over most of the story. 300-year-old Prince Ren falls completely in love with Kelsey, though he feels competitive with his savage brother Kishan. Kelsey relates:

> Ren was like a fantastic jungle waterfall – sparkling and shimmering in the sunlight. He was an exotic paradise waiting to be discovered. Kishan was different. Kishan was a raging, grade six whitewater river – fast, unpredictable, and un-navigable to even the most skilled thrill-seekers. (362)

Ren is cursed to be a white tiger with blue eyes, Kishan is a black tiger. Prince Ren dresses in white, with a carelessly buttoned shirt revealing "a smooth, well-built golden-brown chest" (86). Kishan "was very handsome, but in a darker, more swarthy way then Ren. His skin was antique-bronze, and his hair was ink black, swept away from his face and slightly curled" (194). In the third book, Kelsey is locked in a tower to be rescued, while her tormentor costumes Ren as Prince Charming and Kishan as Robin Hood. This is an excellent metaphor for the clashing personalities. Ren also loses his memory, leaving his brother to demand he won't harm Kelsey. Once again, the mild-mannered Prince Charming becomes a potentially murderous threat, and once again, the heroine is physically unhurt but emotionally devastated.

While polite, Ren is high-handed, tricking Kelsey into a dinner date and threatening to force-feed her from his lap when she wants to leave. When she runs home, unwilling to accept the prince's overwhelming love for her, he buys her a car and a houseful of luxuries. She enters her new cottage to find furniture all arranged, her clothes in the closet, and food in the fridge. The prince has enrolled her in the local university, chosen her classes for her, and left the new books, schedule, and a university sweatshirt on the counter.

One of the largest delusions and one of the hardest to shake is "the fantasy of the 'Magical Other,' the person who is going to enter our life and make it work, make it meaningful and painless" (Hollis 113). This prince who will take care of everything, from the chore of moving to the mental exercise of picking classes is terribly compelling. Allowing this help is infantilizing, allowing the prince to become father, protector, and arbiter of everything. Bella has similar moments in her relationship with Edward, as the vampires buy and install a stereo for her truck, and Edward later buys her a bulletproof car. Her honeymoon is arranged from trip to packing, and like Kelsey, she returns home to find a new fairytale cottage, furniture, and a closet of clothes in her size. It's good to be the princess.

Katniss, by contrast, loathes this sort of treatment. The makeovers and fashions are torture for her as the prep team forces her to undergo treatments like a doll. When District Thirteen arranges her schedule, she ignores it. President Snow's gifts, from roses to wedding gowns, are the most revolting to her. However, Katniss is willing for her prince to take care of her, at least as a mutual partnership. In *Catching Fire*, Peeta supplies her family with cookies, and he brings her bread when he returns to District Twelve at trilogy's end. More proactively, on his first day back, he plants primroses outside Katniss's house, and Katniss allows the gesture. While Gale can supply exactly what Katniss can: the spoils of hunting and gathering, Peeta provides luxuries – the bakery bread young Katniss couldn't afford, fancy decorated cookies she and Prim would watch through the glass. Even when Katniss becomes wealthy, the frosted cookies bring beauty to her life, offering something she cannot create herself.

The Price of Choosing

In *Twilight*, Edward is the fairy prince of the story, the creature of the Otherworld come to spirit Bella away from all she's ever known and become his immortal fairy bride. These ancient tales sometimes end with the young woman being rescued by her human sweetheart and settling down with him, while others leave her in the arms of her fantasy lover forever. Being swept off, every decision made, with no way to return is the perfect fantasy. There can be no turning back or divorce for Bella the vampire. She can spend eternity with her Edward, cared for by a host of vampire relatives and seemingly endless funds. No hard choices need present themselves ever again, and in a true fairytale style, Bella can not only live happily ever after but remain eternally beautiful.

> The simplicity of her desire, and Stephenie Meyer's dogged refusal to allow rational logic to enter her heroine's considerations – has an undeniable appeal. Bella enters adulthood without any tradeoffs and tough decisions. Would that we could all do so....It's not a great quest narrative, but Bella is a blank slate upon which, in classic Mary-Sue fashion, readers can project their own wish for a protected life. (Seltzer 41)

Screenwriter Rosenberg notes:

> It's not just about which boy do I want. It's a lifestyle choice. With Jacob, you'd have an earthbound life, a normal life in some ways with

> family and children. Edward represents the ethereal, fantastical life. That makes for a strong triangle. Frankly, just choosing which boy or girl you want is a little shallow. For Bella, it's a matter of life or death. Literally. (Wloszczyna 3)

When put that way, it's disturbing that Bella chooses death. While Bella's suicidal tendencies come up even more blatantly in *New Moon*, when she repeatedly risks her life to catch a brief vision of Edward, her final choice echoes the same low value on her human existence. With Jacob, Bella could visit her family, attend college, have children. Edward warns her that becoming a vampire like him will mean sacrificing all of this, along with her soul. She remains adamant nonetheless. This indicates a desire for the relationship that will consume every aspect of her personality: the fiery choice versus the safe choice. The metaphor here is sacrifice – giving up everything to be with the one Bella loves. "You only have to risk your life every second you spend with me, that's surely not much," Edward says ironically. "You only have to turn your back on nature, on humanity, what's that worth?" (*Twilight* 305). This choice echoes *Romeo and Juliet* (and indeed, *New Moon* contains many references to the story of the girl who would rather die desperately with her love than marry safe, steady Paris.)

Peeta the gentle baker seems like a milder choice than Edward, as Peeta would never take Katniss from her family. However, Katniss nearly gives her life for him, in the Romeo-and-Juliet moment at the end of the first book. She sets it up to play on viewers' sympathies, but she admits to readers that she isn't entirely sure what she's thinking. This scene indicates metaphorically that Peeta is the one great love who, like Romeo, could eclipse the young heroine's entire world. Katniss repeatedly insists that she and Peeta are "not star-crossed lovers!" (*HG* 135), thus reminding readers that on some level they are. "Peeta and Katniss are from different parts of town, from families that don't associate with each other" (Lem and Hassel 126). Their love is doubly forbidden in the Capitol and the first Games, when Katniss fears she will have to kill him. Only alone in the cave, given permission to protect each other and both survive, can Katniss begin to lower her guard.

Seltzer comments: "Katniss is reactive, responding to her life's debilitating constraints (hunger, persecution, and the fear of death), while Bella behaves as if almost nothing – money, family, safety, concern for mortals – matters beyond the fulfillment of her own star-crossed love story" (41). Katniss, indeed, has many ties outside her love triangle: She loves Prim enough to give her life for her, and Haymitch becomes surrogate family, as Katniss continues to care for him after the rebellion. Likewise, Katniss loves Rue like a sister, even mistakenly thinking of her as Prim after they cuddle at night. Choosing Peeta or Gale is incidental to her, far less important than her survival and the survival of those she protects. As Gale notes, "Katniss will pick whoever she thinks she can't survive without" (*MJ* 329). This is Bella's choice as well. Though Bella lacks strong ties to her family, with distant childlike parents and no younger sibling to defend, Bella risks all in love from nearly the first page, a choice defensive Katniss only makes at series end. Both at last settle down to a life in a glowing meadow beside their gentle princes, in what seems to be today's ultimate teen fantasy.

KATNISS, PROTECTOR OF CHILDREN

Many popular books, such as *A Series of Unfortunate Events* and *Harry Potter*, show clueless adults who don't understand the danger their world faces. It is the children who must break the adults' rules to save the day. Panem is an entire world built around this principle. While kids provide for their families, the adults fight needless wars and punish children in the Hunger Games. For Katniss, adults are untrustworthy and deceitful – she knows she can rely only on herself and those like her. But Katniss does more than survive: she becomes a defender of the helpless, one who challenges and defeats the adults of Panem to safeguard its children.

Through the trilogy, Katniss's mother is notable for her uselessness. Katniss has always been the head of the household, since her father died and her mother collapsed. Katniss admits that she mostly took charge to keep her fragile sister Prim out of the community home that would "crush her like a bug" (*HG* 27). Even when remembering the mine accident itself, she wonders why she and her sister had to search for their oblivious mother, rather than the reverse. Most memorable is her mother's shutdown, as she curls up in bed and allows her tiny children to starve. Possibly she is overcome by trauma, or possibly, given her wealthy upbringing and later passive behavior, she feels entitled to be a child herself and have others care for her.

Fairytale mothers always die (or in modern fantasy are incapacitated), allowing the heroine to thrive. Metaphorically, the all-caring mother of young childhood is not what the questing adolescent requires. The heroine cannot quest with her mother holding her hand – she must find the source of support within herself as she grows. The author of *Women Who Run with the Wolves* adds that a woman's psychic chores include the following:

> Accepting that the ever-watchful, hovering, protective, psychic mother is not adequate as a central guide for one's future instinctual life (the too-good mother dies). Taking on the task of being on one's own, developing one's own consciousness about danger, intrigue, politic. Becoming alert by oneself, for oneself. (Estés 81)

When Katniss's mother proves inadequate, Katniss accepts her mother's tasks as well as her own and grows into a true heroine.

It's Katniss who at age eleven risks her life sneaking into the meadow to hunt. She even brings seven-year-old Prim to help her, as their mother won't budge. Years later, Katniss pushes away her mother's touch. Adults cannot save her, Katniss knows.

Gale is Katniss's only partner; together they are like parents protecting their families. This extends so far that Gale and Katniss have a mutual pledge to care for each other's siblings if one is sent to the Games. Gale points out that they could run away "If we didn't have so many kids," as he puts it (*HG* 9). With so many dependents, they have assumed their parents' responsibilities.

Peeta too is a savior of those weaker than he is, as he rescues Katniss with his two loaves of bread. By contrast, his heartless mother beats Peeta and ignores the starving child who's practically on her doorstep. Peeta remains an artless, childish hero through the trilogy. Even confronted with the Games, he's determined to remain a good person rather than a pawn of the Capitol's adults. His actor, Josh Hutcherson said, "I fell in love with Peeta right away. His self-deprecating humor, his outlook on life, and how he doesn't want things to change him – those things are really a part of who I am as a person" (Egan 26). He's like the best of everyone, a voice of hope and high spirits.

By the time the first book begins, Katniss scavenges meat and plants from the forest daily, while her mother and sister are a pair of dependents waiting at home for the food. All they contribute has been originally supplied by Katniss, who brings her mother healing herbs and gives Prim her goat. Their mother has only her prized dresses to offer – the beautiful past she clings to instead of selling the fine garments for food. Her medical skills are seen used on others, not her daughters. When Gale and Katniss are injured, her mother tends Gale with a cool, professional detachment. But there is no sentiment spared for Katniss. She is just another hysterical loved one, and as her mother considers her, "not a priority" (*CF* 112). Peeta is the one to fetch snow for her eye.

As with many other fictional parents, Katniss's mother is oblivious to Katniss's needs and fears. She assumes Katniss has the flu when she's terrified to descend into the coalmine that killed her father. And in the second book, Katniss tries to hide her trips into the forest to keep her from worrying. Katniss also conceals how President Snow is plotting against her, noting, "I think about how there was no going back after I took over caring for the family when I was eleven. How I will always have to protect her" (*CF* 31).

In *Catching Fire,* Katniss has become a greater provider for the household, bringing her mother and sister to *her* house and feeding them from *her* monthly income as she once fed them her tesserae grain. When Gale finally begins work in the mines, Katniss provides food for his family too. In fact, Katniss becomes food provider for her entire district, as they receive parcels of supplies to celebrate her winnings.

In District Thirteen, her mother once again is a healer but not a nurturer.

While Katniss deals with depression and borderline insanity, it is Prim who stays with her and comforts her, then helps Katniss recover from strangulation while their mother is off working. Sweet Prim is an endless support for Katniss, consoling her when Peeta is captured and considering how to undo Peeta's programming. Katniss's memories are filled with just the two of them, comforting each other, gathering food together, supporting the family, while her mother is nowhere to be seen. Meanwhile, though her mother changes little, Prim has matured thanks to her sister's harrowing journey: "The combination of that ordeal and that has followed – the cruelty in the district, the parade of sick and wounded that she often treats by herself now if my mother's hands are too full – these things have aged her years," Katniss decides (*CF* 181).

When the rebels win, Katniss and her mother share a room in Snow's mansion, but her mother is "almost never there" (*MJ* 351). Despairing, Katniss decides to kill herself after she kills President Coin to skip the suffering of what the rebels will do to her. The deciding factor is the misery of facing her mother, bidding her goodbye, and leaving her alone in the world. Even contemplating her own death, Katniss is still concentrating on protecting the woman who should have protected her.

Protector of Life

From the first chapter of *The Hunger Games,* the Capitol is revealed as a force for evil, one that forces children to murder each other for entertainment. Collins comments, "In the book, the annual Hunger Games themselves are a power tool used as a reminder of who is in charge and what will happen to citizens who don't capitulate" (Blasingame).

The entire system preys on children. A child can take another's place in the Games, but an adult cannot. Children must sacrifice themselves for tesserae grain to support their families. The Hunger Games are very much set up as an attack on the districts' *children,* not merely the districts themselves. This is an ugly terrorist form of warfare as there is no defense – each year, twenty-three children are killed – by children. Katniss's success in managing to lower that number by one is groundbreaking and a testament to her character. Collins defined one of the book's themes as, "Mess with us and we'll do something worse than kill you. We'll kill your children." As Collins adds, "And the thing is, it was allowed; the parents sat by powerless to stop it" (Scholastic).

As an interviewer pointed out to Collins, "One of the most disturbing aspects of the 'Hunger Games' is that children are forced to murder other children on live TV. I can't think of another series for young people that has so much kid-on-kid violence."

She responded:

> Well, the thing is, whatever I write, whether it's for TV or whether it's

> books, even if I'm writing for preschoolers, I want the protagonist to be the age of the viewing audience. So I'm not going to write a war story for kids and then just have them on the sidelines. If I write a war story for kids, they're going to be the warriors in it. (Margolis)

Katniss's great fear is that her own children will be forced to fight in the Games, and so she resolves never to have any. From the start, even the thought of training other children horrifies her. "It must be hell to mentor two kids and then watch them die," she thinks, realizing with a shudder that this will be her fate if she wins the first Game (*HG* 386). At that moment, she sympathizes with Haymitch and understands how he could grow so cynical. For Haymitch too was once a terrorized child of the Games. After he won, his family and girlfriend were killed to keep him in line. Looking at him, Katniss sees her hopeless future if she can manage to win. "Perhaps the most crucial story told here is the conflict between children and the adults they may become," Sarah Outterson Murphy comments in her essay on child soldiers in the series, as indeed, the lawmakers have left Katniss only a choice between evils (199).

Nonetheless, Katniss protects other wounded children in the Games. When tiny Rue crosses her path, Katniss lowers her bow, smiles, and offers an alliance. A twelve-year-old girl, even one as capable as Rue, merits her protection on sight. She reminds Katniss of Prim but also of her younger self – Rue is the oldest in her family, used to protecting and feeding her younger siblings. She's always been starved, but she's become talented at foraging and ducking the guards.

Katniss cannot watch suffering, in her mother's patients, in starving children, in the Avoxes. She's drawn to invalids and other helpless people, distributing food through District Twelve as soon as she has enough to spare. Upon seeing the elderly and drug-addled participants in the games, she reflects that "a lot of them are so damaged that my natural instinct would be to protect them" (*CF* 234). She chooses Beetee and Mags for allies, some of the least competent competitors, because they seem to need her.

Katniss's relationships are likewise defined by protecting those who are suffering. In the Games, Katniss finds Peeta badly wounded, and cares for him, not just for the sponsors, but because she can't stand his agony. Her kisses, though also meant for the sponsors, are a tool to convince Peeta to eat and drink. Gale too notes that Katniss only kisses him when he's in pain. In the forest back in District Twelve, Katniss persuades Gale that they both must lead their families into the wilderness, insist, or even drag them by force, as it's the only way to keep them safe. However, her fear for Prim stops her.

At the same time, Katniss realizes that Prim, starved and miserable, has already suffered because of the Capitol. She has seen her father killed and her sister tortured in the Games.

> Prim...Rue...aren't they the very reason I have to try to fight? Because what has been done to them is so wrong, so beyond justification, so evil that there is no choice? Because no one has the right to treat them as they have been treated? (*CF* 123).

When Prim tells Katniss she's going to be a doctor, "Something small and quiet, like a match being struck," lights up the gloom (*MJ* 150). This is what Katniss has been fighting for: A better future for Prim and all the other children. It's no accident that Rue and Prim die in the war. Of all the characters, they are the most innocent, sweet, and helpless, a reminder to readers that those who deserve it aren't always the victims. It's the civilians, even the youngest, who starve and die when one country attempts to prey on another.

KATNISS AS CHILD

Katniss is really just a teenage girl – as such, her youth and purity are frequently emphasized. Katniss "is a character for whom gender performance is more or less devoid of sexuality" (DeaVault 193). Her mother's calling her too young for a boyfriend is accurate, as Katniss feels only the first glimmerings of responses to the kisses of Gale and Peeta. Katniss's relationships with both are chaste. In their cave together, Katniss and Peeta share the sleeping bag, but Katniss only thinks of Peeta's arms as warm and protective like her father's. On their victory tour, Katniss invites Peeta into her room simply to hold her and chase the nightmares away. He comments that the other victors like to tease her because she's so "pure," a figure of innocence rather than sensuality (*CF* 216).

She fights through the first book not to defeat the Capitol, but simply to play the game they've designed for her and survive it. When she wins, the Capitol's helicopters carry her off, paralyzing her as they do each time to demonstrate their power and her helplessness. The medical staff pours her a glass of orange juice, like a preschooler's reward for playing nicely with others. And Katniss congratulates herself not for defeating the Capitol but for doing as she's been told and giving the people a wonderful Game.

> For the two books leading up to "Mockingjay," Katniss acts decisively and often effectively, but only when she's backed into a corner. She's forced to participate in the games; compelled to act out a romance with her fellow tribute, Peeta, for the viewing audience and strong-armed into the publicity campaign expected of victors by threats against those she loves. Her behavior is understandable, but never freely chosen. "I'm not just a piece in their game," is her habitual refrain, but except for a few climactic and highly circumscribed moments, she's often just that. What does Katniss really want? It's hard to say. (Miller)

In *Catching Fire,* Katniss's status as child becomes clear. President Snow despises Katniss, as she puts it, "because I outsmarted his sadistic Hunger Games, made the Capitol look foolish, and consequently undermined his control" (*CF* 18). This last sounds like Katniss showing up an overcontrolling parent. Indeed, he treats her like a rebellious child, threatening her with punishments and intimidating her. Katniss in turn vows to do whatever he says in order to keep her family alive. Far from rebelling, she submits completely to authority. But her efforts are useless.

Returning to the Hunger Games, Katniss once more is a child in everyone's eyes. All the older tributes conspire with Haymitch (and *not* Katniss or Peeta) to break through the Games and escape. "The less you knew, the better," Haymitch says unapologetically (*CF* 386). Beetee is secretive, Finnick manipulative, Johanna violent, all to make Katniss and Peeta follow their grand plan. And worst of all, while they rescue Katniss to take to District Thirteen as their mascot, Peeta is captured. Once again, the adults have failed to protect those in their charge.

The District Thirteen helicopters carry her to their choice of destination, like parents arriving to heavy-handedly pick up their children from playtime. In the rescue attempt, Katniss lies stunned, unable to move. Following this, she's connected to medical equipment, sedated, strapped down. She's become a pawn in this attempt, figurehead rather than fighter. Katniss describes "this elaborate plan in which I was just a piece, just as I was meant to be a piece in the Hunger Games. Used without knowledge, without consent" (*CF* 385). Her very youthfulness hampers her, in a world in which adults take away all her decisions. This leaves her closed off and even passive, unable to improve her life outside the adults' rules.

Peeta, Gale, and sometimes Prim are Katniss's confidantes. The adults are an unsympathetic Other – even Haymitch, her ally, manipulates and bribes Katniss into following his orders, trying to break through her stubborn personality rather than confiding in her. Cinna is supportive and comforting, but he too uses Katniss as a tool of rebellion, dressing her like a doll in carefully-designed outfits.

Plutarch is another manipulative adult. His hunger for biological weapons and other devices too heinous to be used revolts Katniss. He cares only for the big picture – winning, rather than those individuals killed to bring it about. "Eyes on the forest, not on the trees. Not on Peeta's punishment, or 13's immanent blasting," Katniss notes cynically (*MJ* 140). She's ready to slap him when he commends Peeta's bravery in warning them of an attack, while she can only focus on the punishment he's suffering for it.

After Gale turns eighteen and reaches adulthood, he's still Katniss's best friend, but he's becoming someone new as he grows up – a revolutionary. He trains constantly with the other soldiers, learning how to kill. Worse yet, he designs snares that will murder civilians and even doctors. His callous disregard for life appalls Katniss, who's sure he's crossed a moral line. "Gale's own knife-sharp sense of right and wrong gets increasingly blunted as the tale unfolds," notes Elizabeth M. Rees in her essay "Smoke and Mirrors" (60). Gale finally blows up the entire mining fortress of District Two, pointing out that they are murderers. His own district has been destroyed, so theirs must be, in revenge. When he later defends his actions as a preemptive strike, Katniss responds that any violence, even the Hunger Games, could be defended by what the victims might do someday. Gale has become a revenge seeker, one willing to kill the innocent in pursuit of victory. That viewpoint Katniss, rescuer of the helpless, can never excuse. Throughout the attack, she pictures the mine accident that killed her father, empathizing with the workers of District Two until she risks her life to stop the battle. She is unwilling to fight for the Capitol's agenda any longer.

> If violence in the standard hero myth serves at its core as an allegory for the youth's journey from weakness and victimization to independence and power, then *The Hunger Games* questions the assumption that this journey to adulthood is worth pursuing in such a violent world. (Murphy 199)

Obedient Gale has become what the adults desire – a gleeful killer. This prompts Katniss to follow her own path. The adults have manipulated her through the second Hunger Games and then the rebellion. But Katniss is determined to take charge for herself.

Similar Series

Dystopian YA allows teens to fix problems, giving them far more power to operate than they have in today's world. Veronica Roth, author of *Divergent*, explains, "I also love that the majority of characters in dystopian and post-apocalyptic literature have a lot of agency – they take charge of their lives in environments that make it hard for them to do so, and I love reading about strong characters like that ("Q & A with Veronica Roth," *Divergent* 5). In the U.S., people under eighteen can't vote, can't make legal decisions without a parent or guardian. But dystopian teens can change the world. As Katniss devotes herself to protecting the helpless of her world, she gains control, reminding us we can do the same.

> Most contemporary YA novels focus on small scale concerns: domestic, athletic and scholastic dramas. By showing societies that depend on teenagers acting as adults, authors can put teenage protagonists into very high-stakes and dramatic situations, where the future of society is at stake. (Dobbs)

Some dystopian worlds are structured so teens are at the center, from Games designed for people twelve to eighteen to the situation in *Uglies,* in which all adults are surgically brainwashed into compliance. Panem has far more kid-power than in our own culture. Before age eighteen, Katniss has two fights to the death for her very survival in two different Hunger Games. She's learned hunting, survival training, and finally warfare. She defies President Snow, becomes a revolutionary, and defends freedom as the beloved face of the rebellion. It's a compelling lure.

Many teen dystopias followed the success of *The Hunger Games*, and a significant number of these pit children against adults. As teens master new strengths within themselves, bullies and fellow teens lose importance. The government – shadowy manipulative adults – is the true threat, often hidden behind the scenes. In a world in which teens must follow adult laws and even die in adult wars, the metaphor is all too real. These are powerful fantasies that resonate in our own flawed world.

Divergent is a novel of sixteen-year-olds who must choose one of five factions to follow. Tris picks the Dauntless faction, where she's pitted against other brave teens for a few coveted spots. However, as she battles bullies and cruelty, it becomes clear that more is going on. As her romantic interest, Four, warns her, if it's discovered that she's not a natural Dauntless but is instead uncategorizable – Divergent – those in charge will have her killed. "They don't want you to act a certain way. They want you to *think* a certain way. So you're easy to understand. So you won't pose a threat to them," he explains (Roth 312). Tris is appalled – her fellow teens may scheme and even try to kill her, but at least she knows the rules. The shadowy existence of a mysterious government who will destroy her for being born different is another matter entirely.

Further, Tris, like Katniss, is a protector of helpless children. Tris's childhood training in the selfless faction of Abnegation informs much of her value system. "It's when you're acting selflessly that you are at your bravest," Four tells her (311). She protects frightened, helpless Al and helps Four face his darkest fears in a simulator. The adults, by contrast, have twisted their courageous faction into a place of competition – teamwork is discouraged in favor of beating other teens. Tris discovers a better way. As she cheers her friends and reassures them, she builds camaraderie and friendship, growing from competitors to real teammates.

In *Wither* by Lauren DeStefano, all men die at age twenty-five and women at twenty, thanks to a genetic accident. Only the unaffected generation, those over seventy, age normally. As such, the world is firmly divided into the "first generation" of the elderly and the younger ones with limited lifespan. Sixteen-year-old Rhine is kidnapped to be forcibly married to a wealthy young man a few years older than she is. However, as she soon discovers, he's terribly naive and has no idea girls were abducted and killed to find him brides. It's his father, a first generation, who has orchestrated all this. Worse, as the father experiments to restore normal aging, he's operating on the dead bodies of teen wives and babies, anyone who might aid his research. Trapped in their mansion, Rhine must sneak around him, lulling his suspicions and seeking an escape before she too ends up in his basement of horrors.

Gone is more direct – in an instant, everyone over fourteen vanishes from a small town, and a barrier springs up around it. The bad teenagers like Caine and Orc neglect the children and even threaten to kill them, while the heroes like Sam and his girlfriend risk their lives saving others. However, even the good teens find themselves unable to do more than bury the dead on too many occasions. It's eventually revealed that the adults had let the power plant get out of control, and a single child discovered a way to stop it – using his mental powers to send them all away. A mysterious alien force is also responsible – an evil that takes the shape of Sam's mother, as if the parent-child war wasn't obvious enough. As the first book begins a teen civil war, Sam protests that they can't let nine-year-olds be soldiers and praises his best friend for failing to kill an enemy. However, his attempts to keep peace fail. In a world of only children, there are no innocents left.

Other stories show worlds in which age doesn't matter, only ability. *Feed* tells the story of a deadly zombie virus dismissed by the reputable news until one researcher posted it on his only available channel: his eleven-year-old daughter's blog, decorated with teddy bears. As the book's narrator, a teen blogger and licensed journalist, explains: "People don't trust regulated news anymore. They were confused and scared, and they turned to the bloggers, who might be unfiltered and full of s***, but were fast, prolific, and allowed you to triangulate on the truth" (Grant 49-50). Using the only outlet available, teens are telling the truth and gaining credibility and respect, in a world betrayed by traditional media. Further, one critic notes that virus-based dystopias "are almost never natural in origin. They are either the work of demented governments and hubristic scientists, or, in our era of migrating viruses, a subset of climate change apocalypses" (Bethune). Once again, the adult scientists and consumers have destroyed the world, leaving the teens to save it.

Collins's previous series, *Gregor the Overlander*, also has a major kid power theme. Gregor is a stay-at-home brother, used to babysitting his two-year-old sister while his mom works. When he follows little Boots down a tunnel into the Underland, he begins a quest to find his father, who vanished there two years before. Through their quest, he is Boots' perfect caregiver. He changes her diapers, feeds, and comforts her through every step. It hasn't escaped him that he is the only parent Boots has: "Gregor felt like all the grown-ups had gone home and left the kids....Inside, he felt sick and hollow and very young" (Collins, *Overlander* 215).

On their travels, Boots gets a fever and Gregor wishes fervently for his mother, then determines to find his dad, whom he thinks will "make it all right" (Collins, *Overlander* 235). However, his father is delirious and dazed. Like Katniss, Gregor realizes he can't be a child anymore but must instead care for his unwell parent: "Gregor had thought he would get a parent back when he found his dad. Then he could stop having to make hard decisions. He could just be a kid. But the man before him was even needier than Boots was" (Collins, *Overlander* 259). In the third book, Gregor quests to save their mother, but once again, he succeeds and finds that she can no longer protect him. Both his parents remain ill, and he must bear the caregiver burden in the normal world, not just the magical one:

> If his mom was gone for months, if his dad got bad again and couldn't even take care of them, let alone go back to work and even if he could go back to work, then who would take care of his grandma and Boots and where was the money for all this going to come from, anyway? And whoever he was in the Underland, in the real world Gregor was just an eleven – no, a twelve-year-old kid who had no idea what to do. (Collins, *Warmbloods* 357-358)

Instead of having his parents support them, Gregor is the one to earn money, to find cures for his parents' ailments, to arrange a babysitter. At age twelve, he's become the real man of the house.

Luxa, the warrior queen of Underland, is only twelve. However, in her world, children train as young as six and she's incredibly capable.

> Luxa would not have the full powers of a queen until she was sixteen, but at twelve she had great influence and could now cast votes at the council meetings where policy was decided. While she was stubborn and gave the council fits with her attitude, Luxa was smart, strong, and unquestionably brave. (Collins, *Marks of Secret* 41)

Once she loses her parents, she spends all her days flying with the giant bat Aurora and officially bonds with her in a fighting partnership, far younger than other warriors. When other adults abandon the quest, leaving her with Gregor, Boots, and the talking animals, she becomes a clever leader.

Hazard, age seven, joins the quest of the fourth book. He's skilled in languages of the other races, and it's revealed that only he and Boots are young enough to learn them. When a giant scorpion attacks, Hazard leaps down to protect his bat from death and manages to plead for peace. Between his ability to communicate and Boots' loving effort to pet their babies, the scorpions are convinced and make a treaty.

Far from dead weight, Boots contributes much to their journey in the tiniest example of kid power. When Boots first meets Luxa, the warrior unsympathetically tells Boots that she can only have a ball if she can take it, adding, "You will have to be stronger or smarter than I am" (Collins, *Overlander* 29). Confused, Boots pokes Luxa in her alluring purple eyes, and Luxa drops the ball. Gregor smirks that Boots is clearly smarter. On the quest, Boots loves animals and is utterly fearless, in contrast to Gregor, who panics about flying on bats. She is so kind to the giant cockroaches that they recognize her as a figure of prophecy and become her allies. When they are scared, she sings to them all day to distract them. Repeatedly, it's made clear that the cockroaches only want to fight beside the Underlanders to protect her. Their mentor calls Boots "a natural ambassador" who "treats all with an equality I myself aspire to" (Collins, *Overlander* 196). In battle, she frightens spiders with her loud tantrum. Later, her princess wand serves as their only flashlight and her song gives them a clue to a secret prophecy. Without her, the quests would not succeed.

In the fifth book, Gregor's terrified eight-year-old sister, prone to panic attacks, descends into the Underland. Lizzie has a gift for patterns and logic puzzles, quickly breaking the rats' secret military code. When she sees all the delegates arguing at the negotiation table, she offers the startling idea that each side should only have one delegate...chosen by all the other species. In this way, all the antagonistic voices are banished and the more moderate representatives can make a solid peace. As her friend, the rat Ripred, comments, "Everyone will feel that they have been treated unfairly, but will be happy that their neighbors feel the same. And that is the nature of compromise" (Collins, *Code of Claw* 395). In a very real way, little Lizzie creates the ceasefire.

Boots and Lizzie, like Prim, symbolize the vulnerable childlike side of the hero. Prim is Katniss's reason for offering herself in the Games, for fighting for a better Panem. When Prim is taken from her, she collapses, losing all hope. Only with a way to memorialize all those she's lost in a new book does Katniss begin to reassemble her life. At the end of the series, Lizzie and Gregor have terrible nightmares from the war they've witnessed. Boots is less damaged, though she's learned what death is. Still, she remains hopeful, comforting Gregor with the idea that his loved ones still live on in his heart. Gregor thinks of Boots as a reason to try to improve the world and make it a place of hope, in which people have matured beyond the need for war. He ends the series feeling lost, as if he cannot discover the everyday boy under the scars and trauma he underwent below. However, Boots' last line is to pronounce his name properly for the first time – he may feel lost but she has found him.

Rebellion

Katniss becomes the Mockingjay for District Thirteen, finally supporting the cause she chooses instead of the one forced on her...or does she? No one, even Gale, tells her that Peeta has a television appearance, because no one wants to upset her. Worse yet, President Coin, the new adult authority, is determined to control her. When Katniss demands mercy for her friends, Coin agrees, but she retaliates by torturing Katniss's childish prep team, to remind her that there will always be a way to hurt her.

Through all her time in District Thirteen, Katniss's determination to kill Snow, a selfish thought amidst a world of orders, keeps her going. She defies instructions to try to save hospital victims in District Eight and risks her life to calm the fighting in District Two. But these are only the prelude for her great rebellion.

When Boggs, her benevolent commander, is killed, Katniss finally takes charge. She takes the Holo and refuses to surrender it. When she orders career soldiers to follow her on a desperate mission to assassinate Snow, all agree. At last she's become a leader of adults, not simply a rebellious child ducking orders and trying not to get caught. Katniss is following her own agenda at last...and she's surprisingly capable for a first mission. She leads a diminishing group of soldiers to President Snow's very gates, and nearly makes it inside. And then, Prim is sacrificed before her eyes.

Katniss becomes the Mockingjay to save children like Prim and Rue, but in the end, she fails them both. When she realizes that war will always come, that adults will always sacrifice children to stop their conflicts, she sinks into despair. Once more she lets the adults take charge, hold a trial without her, decide to send her home to District Twelve, send Haymitch and Greasy Sae to care for her as her babysitters, send her mother elsewhere. But gentle Peeta, her fellow victim in the Games, comes to break her out of her depression. Together they memorialize their lost friends, including the youngest.

Following the war, Katniss resists having her own children, even with no more Hunger Games. She knows that the most vulnerable will always be at risk. But she finally agrees to have them, to choose life in a world of death. She retires from the public gaze to be a mother, the greatest adventure of all. "Transitioning to motherhood is a brave decision, both on Katniss's part and Suzanne Collins's," comments Ned Vizzini in "Reality Hunger: Authenticity, Heroism, and Media in the Hunger Games" (97). She can follow her own path, not the one society has forced on her, and find healing. And finally, she sings her children the lullaby she sang to Rue and Prim, expressing her love and her hope for a better world.

Together with Peeta, Haymitch, and the cat Buttercup, Katniss forms a new society. All have lost loved ones, but this new gathering of damaged, lost children, plagued by guilt and nightmares, bonds into a true family, one that can stand together through every moment of sadness. Even laughing young children who play on a graveyard.

KATNISS THE MOCKINGJAY
THE POWER OF STORY AND SONG

Katniss grows up in a world of lies – the Peacekeepers are really killers, the electrified fence is a sham. Her mother warns her to always act properly and obediently, teaching that appearance outweighs reality. Panem is a world of stories and storytellers: the Capitol maintains the fiction that they are in control, and Katniss and Peeta become storytellers powerful enough to take that control from them. Katniss strives to find truth, and as she does, she constructs a new tale. Connecting with her roots, she finds a power beneath that of Plutarch's staged propos – the influence of story and song.

Sacrificial Lambs or Star-Crossed Lovers

Katniss's journey begins with the reaping, which contains the story of Panem, told each year by the Mayor.

> He tells of the history of Panem...a shining Capitol ringed by thirteen districts, which brought peace and prosperity to its citizens. Then came the Dark Days, the uprising of the districts against the Capitol. The Treaty of the Treason gave us new laws to guarantee peace. (*HG* 17)

This propaganda-filled story is clear – the Capitol is "shining" and filled with "peace and prosperity." The districts, through "treason" created the "dark days." Katniss hates the story, whose real message, she knows, is "Look how we take your children and sacrifice them and there's nothing you can do" (*HG* 17). In the movie, the official story of Panem goes on to add the following:

> And so it was decreed, that each year, the various districts of Panem would offer up in tribute one young man and woman to fight to the death in a pageant of honor, courage, and sacrifice. The lone Victor, bathed in riches, would serve as a reminder of our generosity and our forgiveness. This is how we remember our past. This is how we safeguard our future.

The lies here are more blatant: the Games in no way represent generosity and forgiveness: they are a tool of oppression, cruelty and exploitation. Only the last line about safeguarding the future (by threatening the districts into obedience) may be true. "In the book, the annual Hunger Games themselves are a power tool used as a reminder of who is in charge and what will happen to citizens who don't capitulate," Collins notes (Blasingame 726).

Hunger is the day-to-day weapon used to torture the citizens of the districts "as a weapon to control populations," as Collins puts it (Blasingame 726). The Games are the strongest version of that weapon, forcing the districts to watch as their children are starved, tortured, and murdered, turned into the savages the Capitol imagines them to be. This is a truly brutal form of tyranny, aimed at the most innocent and helpless members of society. However, when Katniss takes Prim's place, a moment of truth shines through. The crowd raises their hands in the three-fingered signal once used by Christian martyrs in the Roman arenas. Already, Katniss is telling the districts a new story, one of heroism and rebellion.

In the Capitol, Katniss is asked to tell her own story in the interviews. This is another story told by the Capitol, and Katniss is revolted at the prospect. It is Peeta who truly makes her desirable. His story, like Katniss's, is true, but carefully chosen to play to the audience. Just as District Twelve thrilled at the thought of their self-sacrificing heroine, all of Panem is touched by the star-crossed lovers. "Instead of having a real love story or a real relationship by confessing it to Katniss, he offers it up as fodder for the media, hoping it will help save Katniss's life" (Belviso 3). Haymitch points out that Peeta has made Katniss desirable, and in the film he approaches Seneca Crane to help sell the story of "young love" to the public. In the Games, Katniss makes the star-crossed lover story work, acting as if in a play, imitating the gestures she saw between her parents. And the story sells.

The movie, however, is more nebulous on whether Katniss is acting: Her scenes in the cave, her attempted suicide, may be viewed as real. As a critic in *Ms. Magazine* notes:

> In the book Katniss is reluctant to perform romance, let alone pursue it, but in the film she takes to it all too readily, not even flinching when she receives a reprimanding note from Haymitch Abernathy (Katniss's alcoholic mentor) after her first peck on the lips with Peeta: "You call that a kiss?" The book, in keeping with its exploration of performance, voyeurism and spectacle, prompts us to question Katniss's motives and feelings regarding romance: she can be read as strategically acting the part of besotted female. The film, however, loses this more postmodern exploration, offering instead Katniss and Peeta as true star-crossed lovers. (Wilson)

In *Catching Fire*, Snow insists that Katniss continue playing the part of lovestruck teen. Her feelings are irrelevant, he explains, but the *perception* of them could get her killed or save her. Once again, Katniss sells the story, all too aware of the film crew beside her. "My face breaks into a huge smile and

I start walking in Peeta's direction. Then, as if I can't stand it another second, I start running. He catches me and spins me around" (*CF* 34). There is no emotion, only careful playacting, as if she's summarizing a television show, or playing a part on one.

Peeta is better at charming viewers. Katniss notes, "He can use words. He obliterated the rest of the field at both interviews. And maybe it's because of that underlying goodness that he can move a crowd – no, a country – to his side with the turn of a simple sentence" (*CF* 235). Peeta not only gathers sympathy for Katniss with his revelation that she's pregnant, but he charms the audience, asking sweetly if they can all keep a secret and reluctantly spinning out his falsehoods to win them over. Once more, Katniss is angry and shocked at their roles in the story: she is the helpless romantic figure and he, the loving protector. Though she maintains Peeta's ever-growing fiction, she finds herself increasingly confused how her feelings would develop without the staged romance. She's losing herself in the star-crossed lovers tale.

By the third book, her romance is acknowledged as fake, especially within District Thirteen. Coin brutally asks if Katniss wants to present Gale on camera as her "new lover." Plutarch responds as if they're making a movie, saying, "I think we should continue the current romance. A quick defection from Peeta could cause the audience to lose sympathy for her" (*MJ* 33). Later, he disposes of her fake pregnancy with a line of dialogue. Katniss responds to all this with annoyance, at least inside her head, thinking, "The very notion that I'm devoting any thought to who I want presented as my lover, given our current circumstances, is demeaning" (*MJ* 34). Though the romance was necessary to save her life, it's hardly something she obsesses about on her own. Aloud, however, she meekly agrees and allows District Thirteen to cast her as their Mockingjay.

PRIM'S TALE, RUE'S TALE

Katniss remains aware that she's watched at all times, so she creates her stories accordingly. In the cave with Peeta, she honestly tells the story of Prim's goat, offering up Prim's joy as a way of bonding with Peeta and her listening audience, but she censors how she got the money for it. Meg Belviso, author of "May the Narrative Be Ever in Your Favor: Storytelling in The Hunger Games" explains: "A family heirloom says: I am noble but poor. A deer says: I break the Capitol's laws and it pays" (3). In her inner monologue, Katniss sees herself as the always-capable provider of food, the one who protects her family from starvation: Prim's goat, her illegal hunting, the grooslings she brings down and gives to Rue and Peeta: all are a sign that she is the feeder of others, always in control. Thrown as she is into the *Hunger* Games, this is an important symbol. Katniss, like Rue and Thresh, can gather food and endure hunger. The Career Tributes can do neither. As she reminds Rue and Peeta she's a survivor, she is speaking to the watching eyes of the audience, reminding them that she's the most likely to endure.

Nonetheless, when she sings to Rue, she's thinking of the girl, not the cameras. Her song paints the beautiful meadow, the real place that means safety and beauty in her life. With her lyrics, she creates an image of safety, hope and love, the same place she offers to Prim and her own children, the other sweet innocents of the story. The story Katniss tells herself has become muddled – in her head, she has confused Rue and Prim, seeing Rue as the innocent sister she's always protected. This adds an extra poignancy to the death, and foreshadowing for what's to come.

Only after the song ends, does Katniss drape Rue in flowers to send a message to her viewers. Draping her creates her most defiant story in the Games: She makes everyone see Rue as beautiful and beloved, a young girl sacrificed. Rue was not merely a pawn in their games, and neither is Katniss, protector of the helpless. As she notes:

> I want to do something, right here, right now, to shame them, to make them accountable, to show the Capitol that whatever they do or force us to do there is a part of every tribute they can't own. That Rue was more than a piece in their Games. And so am I." (*HG* 167)

Katniss reminds District Eleven that they all have free will even in the midst of horror. District Eleven responds that evening, sending her a silent thanks with a gift of bread. Belviso notes:

> By respecting Rue, Katniss has done what Rue's district wished they could do. She's acted for them. Instead of just watching passively and helplessly, they can identify with Katniss. In short, they begin to relate to her like the hero of a story. (8)

The film carries this further: though the book is from Katniss's point of view and can only show the wordless gift of bread, the film shows District Eleven returning Katniss's three-fingered salute and rebelling against the Peacekeepers. They begin the revolutionary war of the series urged on by Katniss's gesture and the knowledge that Rue was, as Katniss has framed her, a beautiful helpless pawn in the Capitol's cruelty. In *Catching Fire,* Peeta paints Rue to tell the same message: that of a sweet innocent killed for entertainment. Katniss decorates a dummy and hangs him to tell a more chilling story: that of the dead Gamemaker who died at Snow's pleasure. With flowers and paint, a rope and a song, Katniss fans the early flames of discontent.

THE GIRL WHO WAS ON FIRE

Katniss lights the fire of revolution, from the first moment she dazzles spectators with her flaming costume in the opening procession. She continues to burn in her jeweled ballgown and yellow candlelight dress, until all who see her are consumed by her passion. However, Katniss doesn't create any of this. Cinna is the designer, who in the book requests District Twelve far in advance and designs the costumes before even meeting her. He plans to make its tributes "unforgettable," even before meeting Katniss and Peeta (*HG* 66). In the world of stories and propaganda, Cinna creates a tale of the underdogs from District Twelve who nonetheless outshine everyone. But that makes it his story, his revolution, not Katniss's. She's just his model.

In the movie, Cinna compliments Katniss's bravery in trading herself for Prim and seeks to reward her for it. "I just think somebody that brave shouldn't be dressed up in some stupid costume, now should they?" Here, it's clearer that he's aiding Katniss for herself. Of course, in both versions, his genuine affection grows, and he makes the candlelight gown to cast her as a foolish girl who's "innocent" and "harmless" with more romance than sense (*HG* 355). Here his costume is made to help Katniss personally, keeping her alive rather than exciting more rebellion.

In the second book, Cinna designs Katniss's mockingjay gown, but doesn't even tell her she's wearing it. As Katniss twirls, fire and smoke transforming her from the Capitol's puppet bride to a rebellious mockingjay, this isn't her message, it's Cinna's once more.

Cinna's flames are all artificial, emphasizing the fakeness of it all – Katniss is not really the proud District Twelve representative burning like flame or the glamorous teen glittering like Miss America in her interviews. However, as she puts on Cinna's costumes, she begins to grow into both these roles. The audience sees her as glittering heroine, and as they loudly admire her, that's who Katniss becomes.

By the third book, Katniss claims her role as not only Mockingjay and rebel poster girl but girl on fire. Beetee designs her fire bow, which she uses to defend a hospital and shoot down enemy hovercraft. Afterwards, she announces to the camera, "If we burn, you burn with us" (*MJ* 106). This line, not scripted or fed to her, becomes another symbol for the rebellion.

Fire is mesmerizing, enticing, powerful. But it is also destructive, and like Gale's fiery rage, it can burn friends and allies as well as the enemy. The second book's title, *Catching Fire,* is a metaphor for the spreading energy of the revolution. Katniss is no longer merely trapped in a game; she is becoming something powerful and uncontainable. Her message of rebellion is spreading through the districts like, yes, a wildfire. However, firebombs raining from above are what destroy District Twelve at the book's end. The fire of revolution turns destructive, destroying the innocent as well as the soldiers.

"You're not afraid of fire, are you, Katniss?" Cinna asks prophetically (*HG* 67). In fact, fire is Katniss's enemy – it burns her horribly in the Games, as a

Gamemaker's tool she cannot defend against. Likewise, flames take Prim from her in the third book. Once again, fire destroys Katniss's world, leaving only ashes behind. Once again, she and her loved ones must rise from the flames and make a new start. This time, however, Katniss experiences a rebirth, rising from fever dreams and horrific injuries to imagine herself with "feathers of flame," like a phoenix (*MJ* 348). Her temporary death, like the phoenix's, lets her rise more alive than before.

Of course, Peeta and Gale share her fire symbolism. Though he isn't called this, Peeta dresses as "the boy on fire" in the chariot procession and wears colors to match hers in the interviews. Katniss reflects that he should know a lot about fire, as he works with bakery ovens. Gale too has a fiery temper. However, as Katniss tells her readers, "What I need to survive is not Gale's fire, kindled with rage and hatred. I have plenty of fire myself" (*MJ* 388). To her, Peeta is a dandelion, her symbol of hope. Dandelions, of course, are as yellow as her candlelight dress, with pointy petals like a sun's rays. They resemble a kind of fire, but a tiny, natural, life-sustaining one. They feed people rather than destroying them. And whether it's bread ovens or life-sustaining dandelions, Peeta's flames are an image of food and comfort. Gale, as his name suggests, is a destructive storm wind, the firebomb that kills innocents as well as soldiers. The two kinds of fire they offer tug Katniss in different directions as she decides whether to be cruel or kind, burn the world to pieces or help it to heal. Fire is a destructive force in her life, but also a fierce one. Only she can decide how to direct it.

KATNISS'S MOCKINGJAY

"The symbol of the mockingjay means something very different depending on who is giving and receiving it. It works, in other words, a bit more like a story" (Belviso 4). Collins notes:

> Now the thing about the mockingjays is that they were never meant to be created. They were not a part of the Capitol's design. So here's this creature that the Capitol never meant to exist, and through the will of survival, this creature exists....Symbolically, I suppose, Katniss is something like a mockingjay in and of herself. She is a girl who should never have existed. (Margolis)

Mockingjays are tiny birds that escaped the Capitol's control and adapted to survive, much like Katniss. She of course, is the girl from the poorest district, the one never expected to win. But she does, and like the Mockingjay, she embarrasses the Capitol with her very existence. The Capitol, as Katniss thinks, never counted on the jabberjay being able to slip their control, to adapt, to thrive and mate in the wild. "They hadn't anticipated its will to live," she concludes (*CF* 92). Mockingjays aren't fighters, but hidden survivors, much like Katniss who sneaks into the forest to hunt and wins the Games with humble arrows and apples as her weapons. Katniss comments, "I am the mockingjay. The one that survived despite the Capitol's plans. The symbol of the rebellion" (*CF* 247).

Both girl and bird are kind of hybrid. Katniss's mother comes from the upper class and her father from the Seam. She is a child and a breadwinner, a pawn and a revolutionary, a young girl and a warrior. Further, the mockingjay isn't a construct but a natural product of its environment. Like Katniss, it wins admirers with sweet songs and independence, not by doing what the Capitol intends.

Birds are creatures of heaven and spirituality, like angels. Mockingbirds are so-named because they playfully imitate other birdcalls. Of course, a mockingbird in particular evokes *To Kill a Mockingbird:* in this book, the bird represents the innocents who do nothing but make the world sweeter but are sacrificed without reason. This is a strong theme in *The Hunger Games* as well. Mockingbirds and bluejays both fight viciously to protect their nests.

The Mockingjay is set in a golden ring. The circle is a feminine symbol "associated with the idea of a protected or consecrated space" (Walker 4). It symbolizes matriarchal rule with a circle of equals rather than a patriarchal hierarchy. This is the world Katniss fights for as she becomes the Mockingjay. As she walks into battle wearing a tiny, perfect golden world over her heart, she's fighting for a better future, even as she comes to learn that world doesn't exist.

Certainly, Katniss responds to the symbol and embraces it for herself. Rather than discarding the pin beside her mother's dress, she wears it proudly into the Games. Mockingjays are personal to Katniss – her father loved them and taught her to sing with them. However, like Cinna's flames, the symbol is assigned to her: Madge offers it, as we eventually discover, because it had belonged to her aunt Maysilee Donner, who, like Rue, died helping a stronger District Twelve tribute win.

Rich girl Madge, her bedridden mother (Maysilee's twin), and sacrificed Maysilee herself are all Mockingjays, voices of strength despite the Capitol's tyranny. Madge may have given Katniss the pin as a symbol of District Twelve pride, with the message that subtle, forest-dwelling mockingjays can sometimes triumph. It may simply be the best thing she has to offer, a gift for her friend. Or it may be a signal to Haymitch: He and Maysilee were allies in their Game. Though Maysilee nearly made it to the end, she perished wearing the pin, and Haymitch could only hold her hand as she died. Madge likely grew up hearing this family tale of courage and sacrifice. Putting the pin on Katniss may be designed to wake feelings of guilt and responsibility in Haymitch and jolt him from his drunken stupor. If this is the case, Madge saves Katniss's life.

Madge and the first part of Maysilee's name, May, come from Margaret (meaning pearl), as does the name Mags, casting them all as pearls – symbols of hidden value. Effie Trinket points out in a ludicrously incorrect statement that the children of District Twelve may surprise people because "If you put enough pressure on coal, it turns to pearls" (*HG* 74).

> Granger notes the pearl symbolizes "genius in obscurity," or undiscovered talent across the world because the precious gem is hidden within the secret chamber of an oyster ("Unlocking 'The Hunger Games'"). Mags and Madge, whose names mean pearl, both come to embody this quality. By the time Peeta gives Katniss a tiny pearl in *Catching Fire*, she's come to realize that he too has value below the surface...These pearl characters shine like beacons, guiding Katniss to see how Snow's tyranny affects even the privileged, even those who seem witless or clownish: All these people can be heroes in the end. (Frankel, *Katniss* 74-75)

The film rewrites the story of the mockingjay pin, likely for time, and creates a different symbolism. Katniss herself gets the pin at the Hob and presents it to Prim, saying, "It's a mockingjay pin. To protect you. And as long as you have it, nothing bad will happen to you." The symbol of defying the Capitol has become one of protection (though these concepts are certainly linked – only running from the Capitol produces any safety). Prim in turn presents it to Katniss so it will protect *her*. As such, the pin comes to represent the love between the two sisters, like an angelic blessing of sheltering wings. It's no wonder that Rue reaches out to Katniss, the loving savior of her little sister.

In fact, angel symbols are sprinkled throughout the film, from Katniss and Peeta's flaming wings to Rue's District Eleven costume with a silver wreath of grain like a halo. Katniss's silver-feathered arrows and the white feathery flowers that surround Rue. When Rue dies, a beautiful light shines and she goes still. They tell us, the Games' other audience, a tale of goodness and innocence amid the worst of humanity's brutality.

To Katniss, Rue will always be a tiny bird, arms spread as if to take flight. She continues to wear her pin for herself, and for all the story's lost mockingjays.

The Rebellion's Mockingjay

In *Catching Fire*, Snow's new story is the destruction of hope: All who survived and beat the odds will be murdered. As Katniss notes, victors are "the very embodiment of hope where there is no hope. And now, twenty-three of us will be killed to show how even that hope was an illusion" (175-176) At Snow's demand, Katniss is to be interviewed in her wedding dress, reminding viewers she will never marry her true love. However, Cinna changes this story with his costume. Katniss's gown, like her plans for marriage, burn away, but she rises from the flames as a symbol of rebellion, the Mockingjay. He has recreated her as the one who tricked the Capitol and escaped them, the one whose symbol is being printed on rebel tokens.

Still, the rebels have taken Katniss's symbol and used it without telling her. When she sees the symbol on Plutarch's watch, she doesn't understand. Cinna transforms her dress without her knowledge. Finally, Haymitch organizes a complex escape plan and tells almost all the tributes but his own. Katniss's job as figurehead leaves her only a pawn in the Quarter Quell. Most of the tributes sacrifice themselves for her, but they won't even tell her the reason. As Haymitch and Plutarch finally reveal to Katniss, she and Peeta are the revolution. They have to live and be protected...they just don't have to be informed.

Katniss is furious when she discovers this. In the first book, she survived and saved Peeta by learning to manipulate her viewers, show love for Peeta and finally attempt suicide as star-crossed lovers. She was in charge of the narrative. But in the Quarter Quell, she wasn't even aware what the story was. She had thought she was protecting Peeta, perhaps dying as a martyr since Snow would never let her live. Instead, Haymitch and Plutarch have become the new storytellers, convincing the other victors to protect the face of the rebellion and their only hope for Panem. This has resulted in Peeta's capture.

Mockingjay begins with another constructed story – Peeta's first public appearance since his imprisonment. He frames himself and Katniss as pawns, manipulated and used by the rebels. "Neither of us knew anything except that we were trying to keep each other alive," he screams hysterically (24). If he can sell this story, he may be able to save Katniss. She observes that Peeta's an amazing storyteller even without a paintbrush. But as he begs for a ceasefire, she knows it's the wrong answer.

His story convinces her that she needs to counter him – to get on the televisions and tell people to continue the rebellion, to fight and die so no more innocents will be tortured and murdered. She feels the black and white wings Cinna once gave her fluttering at her back, and resolves to become the Mockingjay. Things proceed quickly from there: She's presented with the uniform Cinna designed, casting her once again as the mannequin in his plans. Beetee has designed a matching bow, though both he and Cinna designed their work to be functional. For her first propo, Fulvia dictates an entirely fake script of how Katniss has fought in some vaguely-defined battle and seen all her nameless comrades killed. To rally the living, she must shout an overly-scripted line Katniss can't take seriously. Haymitch calls her performance "how a rebellion dies," (72) because Katniss is a teller of true stories, not weak constructions.

Peeta is a brilliant storyteller because his moments are framed by truth, from his feelings for Katniss to his idealism. Even his constructed story about their marriage and pregnancy is born out of honest desperation – this is his ultimate fantasy and his best chance to keep her safe. Similarly, Haymitch prompts the rebels to "think of one incident where Katniss Everdeen genuinely moved you…where *she* made you feel something real" (*MJ* 74). The list is especially touching because it's the same list that has moved the readers, Katniss's other, more silent viewers, through the moments of the first two books: Her volunteering to take Prim's place at the reaping, the song she sang to Rue, her drugging Peeta so she could risk her life to save his, her attempt to carry Mags to safety and most of all, the moment with the berries. They mean something different to each person, as Katniss's bravery built a story of defiance, love, and hope: "Love for Peeta. Refusal to give in under impossible odds. Defiance of the Capitol's inhumanity" (*MJ* 75). None of these moments, except perhaps the berries, were meant for the camera. All were Katniss's desperate attempts to save her friends out of love. Plutarch and Thirteen's other storytellers soon realize that people respond to Katniss's genuine heroics, not their flimsy scripts.

In District Eight, Katniss likewise ignores the cameras to bond with the people who are suffering and dying for a free Panem. When the hospital is attacked, she defies orders to enter the battle – in a pinch, she will always try to save lives, not worry about how she looks to others. In her rage at the death of innocents, she shouts her feelings at Snow in a perfect soundbite: "If we burn, you burn with us!" (*MJ* 100). This is her real reaction, and also the story she wants others to hear – Snow is a murderer and Panem must rise against him. She's so caught in emotion, she's stunned when Cressida shouts "cut."

Back in Thirteen, she watches the heavily edited broadcasts. They're a work of art, with close-ups, amazing shots, fade outs, and sound bites. They're better than reality – they're a show as artificially constructed as the Games themselves. But at the heart of both is real death, suffering, and anger, real emotion. Katniss has become as expressive as Peeta. Coin indulgently plays the show twice for her command staff, who applaud as if it's a touching movie. Katniss considers that this is a program new to television, one that will inflame the districts.

Plutarch has become the new storyteller, with his success defined "by the overall success of the production." Katniss even notes that Plutarch will "take his bow" when the war is won (*MJ* 110). For they are constructing a new kind of story, one with the heroic rebels and the evil Capitol, countering the story the Capitol has told from the beginning. "At the beginning of the books the districts of Panem can only see themselves as players in the Capitol's narrative. Through Katniss, they come to believe they could be the heroes of their own stories" (Belviso 1).

In District Two, she speaks to one man and the cameras beyond him, pleading with him to recognize Districts Two and Twelve shouldn't fight – the Capitol is the true enemy. Once again, the heartfelt story she offers to the people around her is inspired and persuasive. Soon enough, it becomes reality.

OTHER STORIES

In the ruins of District Twelve, Katniss sings "The Hanging Tree" for the mockingjays and wounded, voiceless Pollux. She doesn't even realize the cameras are on, as once again, she becomes a storyteller.

> "The Hanging Tree" itself is subversive as it stresses that a man is executed because "they say [he] murdered three" (*MJ* 123). In the Capitol's world of lies and scapegoating, there's no evidence he actually did it. His lover, who may not have committed any crime, is sentenced to die as well, like the executed friends and families of some Tributes. Finally, the ending stresses that death is the only freedom in their dystopian world. (Frankel, *Katniss* 69)

Like her lullaby to Prim and Rue, her song recreates the world into the one she sees, in this case, one of subversion and death.

> This song also becomes an echo of Katniss and Peeta's relationship as each offers him- or herself as a sacrifice in the Games and begs the other to run. They both wonder if death is the only possible end for their doomed romance, beginning with their attempted suicide at the end of book one. Katniss thinks of the song again when Peeta wants to take nightlock in the Capitol: "For some reason, the last stanza to 'The Hanging Tree' starts running through my head. The one where the man wants his lover dead rather than have her face the evil that awaits her in the world" (*MJ* 291). Though she resists letting Peeta sacrifice himself, she finally agrees that he should carry a nightlock pill so he can save the mission and avoid torture at Snow's hands. Peeta stops Katniss's suicide later, telling her she is the only source of hope in his life. As each saves the other, they find ways to keep a flickering hope alive for freedom, even in the midst of horror and trauma. (Frankel *Katniss* 70-71)

While this appears a hopeless song, Katniss is reminding herself that there's always a way to escape the Capitol's cruelty, always a love and trust that can last even beyond death. This is a story she carries with her through the rest of the book.

A more important story Katniss creates is an outright lie. She rushes into combat in Districts Eight and Two, both times without authorization. The first time, she is startled to find that everyone has covered for her, from Boggs to Haymitch. In her invasion of the Capitol, this emboldens her to construct her own larger fiction: She is under secret orders to assassinate Snow and must take charge of her military unit. The fiction holds. Katniss has finally become a strong enough storyteller to make her lies convincing. In fact, Katniss discovers later that the team weren't fooled, but followed her anyway, out of faith. Katniss is legend and storyteller at once, with the power to rewrite her story as she desires.

Gary Ross explains, "the emotional core of the piece is Katniss's long arc from someone who refuses to trust and has to fight for her own survival... versus someone who grows to understand her own humanity and compassion" until she'd rather die than sacrifice someone else ("Casting: The World is Watching"). This is her story of star-crossed lovers with nightlock berries but also the story she spins to Coin, promising obedience until she can kill Panem's new dictator and save the Capitol children from the Games. Once again, others' stories save her, casting her as an emotionally devastated teen not in charge of her actions. Doctor Aurelius covers for her through her trial and after, maintaining the fiction that he's treating her. He, like many, uses the power of story to save the Mockingjay.

As she goes through this quest before the cameras of Panem, the people grow to love her. Her particularly touching moments are ones of sacrificing herself to help Prim, Rue, Peeta, and the other innocents of Panem. However, as Katniss learns compassion, she also learns what Peeta instinctively knows: the amazing power of storytelling.

Of course, we the book's readers and movie's audience are also part of the narrative. We, like the District Twelve citizens, endure the lies of the Capitol propaganda film, and then smile tearfully as Katniss volunteers. Some theatergoers may even have held up three fingers in tribute. Like the Capitol audience, we cry as Katniss sings to Rue and cheer when she hugs Peeta in her candlelight gown. When Katniss's friends recount her best Mockingjay moments, they remind us that we, like them, have been watching her story unfold. On a darker note, we are also the ones desensitized to violence, who watch suffering and injury hoping for entertainment. In this world of narrative, Katniss's job is to charm her audience, both real and fictional, and rouse them to change the world

Collins's message is clear – real war, real anger, real compassion are the stuff of legends. Why does her fictional book move us so? Because the issues she writes about are equally real. The suffering and trauma of child soldiers, the guilt of those who survive, the agony of starving families around the world: All these are real. Collins's narrative is a heartfelt plea to stop ignoring the violence and pain on the news, to hear her call for action and end the violence.

KATNISS THE TEEN SOLDIER

"Something is significantly wrong with a creature that sacrifices its children's lives to settle its differences" (*MJ* 377). This thought of Katniss's is a central theme of the series, reminding readers that in every war, young teens die and the world continues, violent and heedless as ever.

Our modern wars are never fought by the people who make the laws and policies but by the young people – soldiers trained and often drafted at eighteen and nineteen in the US and younger in other parts of the world. Collins addresses this chilling unfairness in her series, showing President Snow safe in his mansion during the Mockingjay War as he and Coin make speeches on television screens. Likewise, Capitol citizens watch the Games for entertainment but lead the safe lives of the rich, knowing the conscription to fight and die will never reach them.

Collins adds:

> One of the reasons it's important for me to write about war is I really think that the concept of war, the specifics of war, the nature of war, the ethical ambiguities of war are introduced too late to children. I think they can hear them, understand them, know about them, at a much younger age without being scared to death by the stories. It's not comfortable for us to talk about, so we generally don't talk about these issues with our kids. But I feel that if the whole concept of war were introduced to kids at an earlier age, we would have better dialogues going on about it, and we would have a fuller understanding. (Margolis)

In 2001, it was estimated that there were 300,000 soldiers under eighteen in the world. As many as forty percent may be girls. Further, they are mostly the children of the poor, as these are the easiest to recruit, the most desperate. "The adults who start and guide the war, or the local commanders who implement it, use children as soldiers because doing so is convenient and cheap" (Wessells 2). Across the world, child soldiers are commonly described as "cheap and disposable," like mine workers or slaves – when they soon die, they can easily be replaced.

Children are particularly vulnerable to manipulation, allowing some to be persuaded that they have no choice but to kill the enemy. Newly conscripted youngsters are told that they must take revenge on the killers of their families, that fighting will end their poverty, or even that dying in battle will send them to heaven. Others take hazardous risks because they don't know better. Teenage boys take on dangerous missions to show off their machismo and impress their peers. The Career Tributes are Collins's strongest example of this last. Their entire lives they are encouraged to fight and win glory for themselves and their districts, leaving them savage brutes willing to murder small children. They may be the greatest victims of the Games.

Today in the US, about half a million high school students are enrolled in the Reserve Officers Training Corps (ROTC) and more join after graduation, in return for college tuition and training. Enlisting young is a way of life, a popular choice for a better future. However, many of those teens die or are permanently wounded in combat before that better future can be reached.

Collins's commentary on war, all too sincere and believable, comes directly from her father's influence. As Collins relates:

> He was career Air Force, a military specialist, a historian, and a doctor of political science. When I was a kid, he was gone for a year in Vietnam. It was very important to him that we understood about certain aspects of life. So, it wasn't enough to visit a battlefield, we needed to know why the battle occurred, how it played out, and the consequences. Fortunately, he had a gift for presenting history as a fascinating story. He also seemed to have a good sense of exactly how much a child could handle, which is quite a bit. ("Conversation")

For Collins, war is central to *The Hunger Games*, as it is to her more child-themed *Gregor the Overlander*. She explains: "For some people, both of these series, 'Gregor' and the 'Hunger Games,' are fantasies; some people call them sci-fi. But for me, they're absolutely, first and foremost, war stories" (Margolis). *Gregor and the Curse of the Warmbloods* especially is concerned with the ethics of war. It features Gregor, who, though not quite twelve, is possessed by a fierce battle rage that makes him a devastating warrior. However, the mysterious jungle-dweller Hamnet tells him to sheathe his sword, and grieves that Gregor has become a warrior so young. As it's revealed, Hamnet was a child soldier himself, until his battle strategy in the dazzling Garden of the Hesperides killed everyone on both sides and scarred Hamnet forever. Devastated by this act, he retreated into the jungle, to never again be an instrument of harm. Hamnet was driven mad, and, from that day forth, the golden apple trees were lost, a sign of the innocence of Eden vanished forever. His life becomes a chilling foreshadowing of what Gregor may become.

THE DRAFT

In Panem, teens in the outlying districts are chosen by lot to fight, in order to punish the districts for a war the children did not create, which happened long before they were born. Here, the poor are unfairly disadvantaged, as the only way they can keep from starving is to bargain their futures for tesserae grain – as Katniss reports, "Gale, who is eighteen, and has been either helping or single-handedly feeding a family of five for seven years, will have his name in forty-two times" compared with the mayor's daughter's five entries (*HG* 13). "It's an allegory – an allegory of this imperial power, of this oligarchy of the multi-rich, of this zero point one percent," Donald Sutherland notes ("Gamemaker"). In America, the statistics are similar – the children of rich families may serve, but poor children often regard the military as the only path toward earning college tuition or getting job training. Others, surrounded by gangs or trapped in broken families, see a place to find a sense of self-worth and empowerment.

Some argue that since the leaders' children generally aren't forced to fight, Congress has no reason to end wars quickly. Drew McWeeny, a movie reviewer, notes that kids today "see a country of very very wealthy politicians and people who are well off who are willing to send other people's kids overseas to a war that is untenable for fifteen or twenty years" and thus will connect with the story of *The Hunger Games*. He adds, "I don't think *The Hunger Games* is escapism...I think it's them recognizing that this is the world we live in, exaggerated" ("Gamemaker").

Various draft exemptions in modern times, from married men to students, once again thrust the burden onto the young (in the first case) and those unable to pay college tuition (in the second). In some countries, bribery is common to avoid the draft, when citizens can afford it. The rich are also better placed to take advantage of more general restrictions such as physical and mental incapacity, with better access to doctors and psychiatrists, to say nothing of lawyers and other advisors.

The Civil War introduced national drafts in the US. Probably between 250,000 and 400,000 boys seventeen or under fought for the Union in the Civil War, making up ten to twenty percent of the army (Rosen, *Armies of the Young* 5). Here, once again, the poor were preferred as soldiers. In fact, when a man was drafted, it was legal to pay someone to take his place, or to pay $300 to the government to escape being drafted. Immediately, the draftees were found in two camps – the rich who could pay their way out or the poor who couldn't. Jokes sprang up about highwaymen calling "$300 or your life," for indeed, everyone had to pay one or the other (Schecter 115).

In New York, a great lottery was held, with slips of paper churned in a great cylindrical drum and drawn randomly – the *Daily News* called it the "wheel of misfortune" (Schecter 120). The fact that everyone – black and white, rich and poor – had their names in the drum promoted calm, as everyone was reassured about the fairness of the process (Schecter 120). However, as it sank in which class would be fighting and which buying its way out, the mood turned ugly. The New York City Draft Riots began a few days later, with mobs shouting, "Down with the rich men!" (Schecter 131).

The reaping scene is equally grim. Actor Liam Hemsworth (Gale) describes it, saying, "There were like 400 extras in the same gray clothes – it was like a prison camp. It was hard not to think about if this were real and someone's brother or sister got picked" ("Let the Games Begin"). Protests are forbidden, and the citizens of District Twelve can only acknowledge Katniss's sacrifice with a silent gesture. The system, in which one teenager can take another's place, invites corruption for those who can afford bribes – if Madge had been chosen, and the Mayor offered the starving miners' children a lifetime of wealth, isn't it likely one would have taken the offer to save his or her family?

Children at War

As long as there has been warfare, there have been rules, especially the one that differentiates soldiers from civilians. Targeting the old, infirm, women, and children was considered a great crime only committed by the dishonorable. Today, however, much of this law is no longer followed. Terrorism, the targeting of civilians, is widespread, and many terrorists fade back into the civilian population after their crime has been committed. Instead of chivalry and the warrior's code, ethnic cleansing and genocide are taking over. In World War I, less than ten percent of casualties were civilians; in World War II, the percentage had risen to nearly fifty (Singer 4). Today, civilians make up the overwhelming majority of those killed.

Katniss reacts with shock when she sees a little Capitol girl dead on the street. As she stands frozen, unable to look away from the tiny yellow coat, she mourns the death of a helpless child. A Capitol child, certainly, but Katniss suddenly understands that by killing her, the rebels are no better than Snow.

The *Gregor* series stresses the same concept – Gregor is sent on a mission to kill the Bane – legendary king of the rats. However, when he discovers a terrified baby Bane screaming for its mother, he feels pity and finds a worthy rat to adopt him. It's soon revealed that killing the Bane would have cost Gregor his heart. Later, the Bane grows into a monstrous leader and murderer of the innocent, but Gregor's mentor reminds him that killing the baby Bane still would have been an unforgivable act. Collins humanizes both sides of the struggle in Underland, guiding the reader to sympathize with mama rats protecting their children as much as with the human families. Both her series emphasize that the death of innocents is the greatest war crime imaginable.

Forcing children themselves to kill is no better. As Gregor's world-wise friend Mrs. Cormaci notes:

> "It's like this. You spend your whole childhood hearing about being nice to other people and how hurting someone's a crime, and then they ship you off to some war and tell you to kill. What's that going to do to your head, huh?"
>
> "Nothing good," Gregor said. (Collins, *Code of Claw* 405)

As defined in the 1989 Convention on the Rights of the Child, children are all people under age eighteen (Rosen, *Child Soldiers* 15). The Games, of course, targets only children, as people over eighteen aren't eligible to fight as tributes or even volunteer. Many of these children go nameless: Marvel, whose name Katniss only learns after killing him, the unnamed boy from Three. Katniss never learns Rue's last name or Foxface's first, and Haymitch is the only one to remember decades of underfed District Twelve tributes sent to an early death. All this emphasizes the chilling loss of so many nameless sacrifices through history.

While the Quarter Quell proves an exception to the Hunger Games' preying on children, Katniss is seventeen in that conflict and in the immediate war that follows – keeping the heroine underage emphasizes that this is a book not only about war but about child soldiers and their heartbreaking victimization in war. Prim of course is even younger – too young to serve even as an army medic though she manages it nonetheless. By international law, recruiting children under age fifteen is a war crime, and District Thirteen has the same age limit. Coin breaks not only today's international and moral laws but the laws of her own district to let Prim serve. Her death is the saddest, as the truly innocent child of the tale pays for the war with her life. She is loved and protected in every way possible, a healer and gentle savior of others, but the war still finds her. This is one sacrifice of many that Coin is responsible for, as in the end she bombs Capitol children and condemns others to the Games.

Of course, Snow has done the same, drafting tributes through a lottery and training them to kill other children as young as twelve. "Katniss is the victim of deliberate and calculating adult manipulation of children's violence for political purposes, and she knows it" (Murphy 200-201). By creating this horrific system, Collins is opening our eyes to the fact that similar acts are happening all over the world today.

In three-fourths of combats today, child soldiers are fighting, sometimes as young as six (Singer 6). Eighty-four armed organizations in the world use children fifteen and under in combat; 64 organizations use children twelve and under (Singer 29). Child soldiers are described as "programmed to kill" and "programmed to feel little revulsion for their actions and to think of war and only war" (Rosen, *Child Soldiers* 21). Like Career Tributes, they are brainwashed to think they have no options besides fighting.

> Hoping in many cases for food, clothing, and shelter, a child's decision to join an armed camp cannot be considered a free choice. Children caught up in armed conflict are desperately seeking for a means of survival. Because of their emotional and physical immaturity, children are easily manipulated and coerced into violence. (US State Dept 2004, qtd in Rosen *Armies of the Young* 20)

In Panem, the Careers are indoctrinated young, trained their entire lives to kill others. "Career tributes are overly vicious, arrogant, better fed, but only because they're the Capitol's lapdogs," Katniss remarks (*HG* 161). Alexander Ludwig, who plays Cato, notes, "I like to think that Cato, before he gets into the Games, is kind of popular and charming, but he's always had that violent anger inside of him. When he gets into the Games he gets lost in this whole sick game and he almost goes insane toward the end" (Egan 42). Cato's speech in the movie emphasizes this lack of options, as he cries:

> Go on! Shoot, and we both go down and you win. Go on. I'm dead anyway. I always was, right? I couldn't tell that until now. How's that, is that what they want? I can still do this... I can still do this. One more kill. It's the only thing I know how to do, bringing pride to my district. Not that it matters.

Katniss is less hardened, as she realizes there's an immense difference between shooting animals and people. When she encounters nonviolent tributes like Foxface and Rue, she has no interest in killing them. But even pacifist Peeta admits that he'll kill to save himself. This is the worst tragedy of the Games, turning children into killers.

Admittedly, other cultures have different views on when adulthood begins. Historically, richer societies with leisure time encouraged children to play and wait longer before taking on adult responsibilities. Poorer societies with a younger death rate, however, encouraged marrying young to ensure marrying and having children at all. Katniss mentions that age is a sign of pride in her district, as so few people can outlive mine accidents, starvation, and disease to become elderly. Once again the districts are contrasted with the Capitol. There, even adults play, betting on the Games and shopping for accessories. Katniss considers them mental children, especially Effie, who seems too limited to grasp that Katniss is fighting for her life in the arena.

War brings poverty to the most vulnerable, depriving families of breadwinners and with them, food and care. As villages are bombed and destroyed, refugees lose their possessions, homes, and means of survival. 2001 saw an estimated forty million displaced people in the world, half of whom were children (Wessells 25). Desperate for protection, these lost children are likely to join armies for food and security.

When District Thirteen welcomes the starving refugees from other districts, those young people are eager to fight for the cause. To the refugees from District Twelve, "sick, wounded, starving, and empty-handed," (*MJ* 6) this stronghold seems a miracle of technology with advanced medical care and enough for everyone to eat. The concrete-enforced bunker offers safety they've never known. However, it turns out District Thirteen's reasons for welcoming them are selfish – the district needs new young people to continue their war. Katniss and Gale, like other young arrivals, are expected to show up for combat training and eventually report to the front.

District Thirteen recruits soldiers as young as fifteen, the age at or above which much of the world recruits. However, most countries officially only allow those underage teens to receive training and serve as support personnel – never on the front lines. Coin has become the killer of the helpless, exploiter of displaced, idealistic children whom she sends to die. Young people tend to be more idealistic than adults. Recruiters take advantage of this, offering young teens "opportunities to help overthrow an unjust regime and build a new social system founded on principles of social justice" (Wessells 36). This is just what Katniss believes as she too staggers into the safety of District Thirteen and agrees to be the Mockingjay. But all too soon, she discovers Coin is no different than Snow.

Aftereffects

Peeta notes after suffering through the Games that to murder "costs you everything you are" (*MJ* 23). He's not even eighteen and his innocence is gone. In District Thirteen, people come "of age" at eighteen, but Peeta is still going to be tried before a war tribunal before Katniss bargains for his immunity. Though he is drafted and forced to fight in the first Games, and volunteers only to protect Katniss and Haymitch in the second, he's unfairly branded a despised criminal and a traitor. "The child soldier as an abused and exploited victim of war is a radically new concept" (Rosen, *Armies of the Young* 6). Only since the 1970's or so have international organizations made provisions for the protection and aid of these terribly exploited young people.

After wars end, some child soldiers have trouble reintegrating because they know nothing else. "Children who grow up having learned fighting as their only means of livelihood and survival are likely to continue fighting for more years than adults" (Wessells 3). As such, when the war is over, child soldiers have profound problems fitting into a peaceful world, as they haven't learned to live in one. Many find other wars still going and reenlist, using the only training they've ever received.

The Career Tributes, trained for war their entire lives, can only continue to bully others and brag of their achievements. Many in District Two grow up to be Peacekeepers – likely brainwashed with patriotism until they believe serving the Capitol is honorable and noble. Though the name Peacekeeper suggests goodness, these are really enforcers of the police state. Following Snow's grim policies, they kill a nameless old man and even the retarded child Martin in District Eleven. Though already rich and successful, many career tribute victors volunteer for the Quarter Quell, since they have nothing besides glory to live for. Katniss, who has lived with a loving family and trained in hunting, at least has the outline of a life to fall back on.

Disarmament, demobilization, and reintegration (DDR) intervention programs are intended to bring security and stability to a region after a conflict (Singer 188). After combatants give up their weapons, perhaps in exchange for cash (Disarmament), they are transported somewhere desirable with jobs or education available (Demobilization). Reintegration finds a productive place for them in society. After Katniss is stripped of her killer bow and locked away during her trial, she goes through this process, shipped to District Twelve to resume her precombat life.

Unfortunately, child soldiers are often ignored when these processes begin. Many, upon returning home, find their family and friends shun them for what they've endured and the atrocities they've committed. Like these families, Katniss's mother abandons her, blaming her on some level for Prim's sacrifice. Peeta and Haymitch have lost their families and have nothing to return for. Together, the three of them form a new family, based on their shared suffering.

The trauma of war appears vividly in the series, especially the final book, as Katniss, Finnick, and Peeta all suffer forms of PTSD. This form of emotional devastation, post-traumatic stress disorder, may affect as many as 97 percent of former child soldiers (Singer 194). The haunting image of Katniss and Finnick tying knots all night to avoid thinking is so painful because it rings true, a physical image of the pain they're undergoing. Even after Katniss's happy ending, the pain of the war still resonates:

> There are still moments when he clutches the back of a chair and hangs on until the flashbacks are over. I wake screaming from nightmares of mutts and lost children. But his arms are there to comfort me. (MJ 388)

Physical scars and burns cover Katniss's body, and she remains constantly aware that her children are playing on a graveyard.

"Many child soldiers are forced to use alcohol or narcotics as a way to desensitize them to violence or to enhance their performance." (US State Dept 2004, qtd in Rosen, *Armies of the Young* 20). Though Haymitch isn't shown doing so in the Games, he retreats into a bottle afterwards, never to reemerge.

Katniss considers what his life is like, training doomed children each year, certain that he will watch them die. In war and peace, in District Thirteen or at home, the only certainty is that Haymitch would rather drink than face what he's undergone.

Whole generations of emotionally scarred children contribute to long-term social instability even after the war has ended. In the course of the series, Gale grows from a hunter and provider for his family into a soldier, one who wants everyone in District Two and the Capitol to perish. Katniss watches, aghast, as Gale designs cruel traps for even noncombatants and medical personnel. When the war ends, he works for the new government, almost certainly as a military advisor. His rage remains a part of him as he continues to fight in service to the new government.

At series end, President Coin convenes the last living tributes, those who suffered through the Games. These include mentally-unstable Annie and Peeta, who have undergone personality-altering trauma. And these are the ones who still value life. Johanna and Enobaria may seem stable, but their experiences have left them bloodthirsty, determined to see other children suffer as they have. They are the tortured children, now grown, whom Coin entrusts with Panem's future. By a narrow margin, the Games are reinstated, as the new leaders watch the Capitol suffer, continuing the cycle of violence and revenge against the most vulnerable, the children.

Collins's *Gregor* series repeatedly addresses the emotional toll of war. Hamnet is the most pronounced example – a scarred adult like Haymitch who wants only to live far from any battlefield. But even the most innocent children with the purest hearts suffer through a loss of innocence. When Gregor finally takes up his destined sword in the fourth book, *Gregor and the Marks of Secret,* he knows there will be a price:

> He would fight because he could think of no other option. But what would that mean for him, the warrior? Who would he be...if he survived...Who would he be when he laid down Sandwich's sword? (342-343)

Gregor joins the battle to halt a secret genocide as the talking rats murder the mice with poison gas. This discovery fills Gregor and all his friends with horror.

> Gregor could not make sense of what had just happened. He had seen death before, plenty of it. But nothing like this. It was not just the number of the dead. [...] What had happened to the mice...trapped in the pit...unable to even defend themselves against the gas...not just soldiers but everyone, even the pups...it was murder on a grand scale. It was a massacre. (Collins, *Marks of Secret* 296)

This scene is likely a reference to the Holocaust, in which Nazis murdered civilians with poison gas, in an attempt to wipe out entire ethnic groups. Tragically, the Nazis are only the most famous case in a world of genocide and atrocities.

After witnessing this terrible cruelty, Gregor can no longer bear to lie to his three-year-old sister Boots for the hundredth time and tell her everyone who dies around them is "just sleeping." He admits to her that their friend, a brave and clever bat who is underage herself, has died fighting, and can offer only the consolation that they can keep her close in their hearts. Children are learning about violence younger and younger – those surrounded by war can only be protected from the truth for a short time.

After witnessing the genocide, Luxa, the Underland's twelve-year-old queen, declares war on the rats. She too is damaged by what she's witnessed, enough to make a terrible oath of vengeance. Gregor, himself a warrior, mourns that he can't find the words to dissuade her:

> Hamnet had tried to explain his position on war to Luxa. How it did no good. How innocent creatures died and, in the end, how it only increased the already intense hatred between the rats and the humans. Hamnet had believed that the least amount of violence used, the better.
>
> The things he'd talked about had made real sense to Gregor...Only he did not know how to work his ideas into some kind of argument with Luxa. (Collins, *Marks of Secret* 198)

By the time the war is ended, eight-year-old Lizzie "hardly talked since the war had ended. She just sat with her legs tucked up under her chair, her face thin and sad" (Collins, *Code of Claw* 371). Boots has discovered death. And Gregor is covered with mental and physical scars, certain he has no refuge left. As Gregor becomes, not just a warrior but a soldier, he knows that he cannot return:

> He was never going back to New York, anyway. That had been some laughable dream. How could he go back after all that had happened? After what he had become? Where would a twelve-year-old kid, a warrior, a killer, ever be at home? (Collins, *Code of Claw* 358)

When he arrives in New York, he's haunted by deep nightmares and cannot watch tragedies on the news with the same ignorance and acceptance he once had. What started as a lighthearted adventure series has turned into a haunting cry for an end to war:

> That's what it would take. People rejecting war. Not one or two but all of them. Saying it was an unacceptable way to solve their differences. By the look of things, the human race had a lot of evolving to do before

> that happened. Maybe it was impossible. But maybe it wasn't. (Collins, *Code of Claw* 411)

CONCLUSION

"When I think back, at the center of all this is the question of what makes a necessary war – at what point is it justifiable or unavoidable?" Collins asks (Margolis). To explore her own question, she writes two epics about war, both of which show enormous body counts, but only a temporary peace and a few fragments of wisdom gained as a result. Child soldiers Katniss and Gregor are hideously scarred to the point they reject violence in their lives, determined to spread a plea throughout the world for war and atrocities to end.

"I guess there isn't a rule book for what might be unacceptable to do to another human being," Katniss thinks, when Gale explains his plans for attacking doctors and civilians (*MJ* 186). At the time of writing, America was divided on the issue of torture and other Bush policies in violation of the Constitution and the Geneva Convention. David Levithan of Scholastic adds, "The books were written so much in the heart and the frustration of the Bush era. And so, in many ways, I think, the commentary there is very much written in the last regime" ("Gamemaker"). With Katniss's words, Collins makes her guiding principle clear – war does not justify all levels of brutality. Gale protests that Snow has broken human decency first, but Katniss rejects his argument. The heroes must stand for something, and that must be ethics, even in wartime. Gale is also puzzled when Katniss grieves for her imprisoned prep team. In his eyes, they're the Capitol, the enemy. They prepared Katniss for the Games where she was sent to die. But Katniss sees them as people and pleads for their safety. Her arguments fail as Gale's strategy kills the innocent Prim and costs him Katniss forever.

Plutarch Heavensbee hopes that the people of Panem have evolved into citizens of their world, who will stop the endless wars before they are destroyed forever. But as he adds, "Collective thinking is usually short-lived. We're fickle, stupid beings with poor memories and a great gift for self destruction" (*MJ* 379). Considering that Panem itself survives in a land of a former apocalypse, he may be right to think the worst of people. This is a dystopian saga, beginning after the human race was nearly destroyed. In the third book, several characters warn that if people keep killing, the human race could actually be wiped out. If the citizens of Panem keep recruiting children and training them in war, they will become a society like we are, a society that settles disputes with the deaths of its children.

KATNISS AS GOOD GIRL, KATNISS AS BAD GIRL

Katniss lives under surveillance, knowing every moment is recorded on hidden cameras. As such, she lives two lives: dutiful schoolchild tidy enough to be safe from the dreaded community home versus ragged, starving teen. Obedient citizen versus the real huntress poaching in the forest. Her mother teaches her to only make mannerly smalltalk and never discuss dangerous subjects, even at home. In the Games, verbally fencing with President Snow, or on camera in her interviews, Katniss must keep her "good girl" persona in place to appear likeable and sweet, the opposite of her true feelings. However, all this repression as Katniss watches her words, learns not to sing, remains polite to her Capitol handlers must have an outlet.

In the psychology pioneered by Jung, this is called the shadow – the bottled-up words we wish we could say, the feelings we suppress so we can function politely in society. When one is bottled-up enough, the shadow can spring to life and act without conscious choice. Jung explains:

> Unfortunately there can be no doubt that man is, on the whole, less good than he imagines himself or wants to be. Everyone carries a shadow, and the less it is embodied in the individual's conscious life, the blacker and denser it is. ("Psychology and Religion"131)

The more it's pushed down, the more it springs up. Jungian analyst Clarissa Pinkola Estés, author of the groundbreaking *Women Who Run With the Wolves,* also stresses the need for balance:

> We find that by opening the door to the shadow realm a little, and letting out various elements a few at a time, relating to them, finding use for them, negotiating, we can reduce being surprised by shadow sneak attacks and unexpected explosions. (Estés 236)

Katniss, however, represses so much of her personality that it's seething to break out.

Each time Katniss fails to save an innocent, she snaps. These are her blazing Mockingjay moments: singing to Rue, threatening suicide, warning the Capitol that "fire is catching." Yet these are also her stunning moments of despair, when, unable to save Peeta, she retreats to her hospital bed. Katniss lives with shadow figures like Buttercup and Johanna: bad, angry characters who echo the anger she suppresses. By contrast, there are quiet-voiced victims who express the gentler impulses Katniss has buried: Rue, Prim, and Pollux teach her to sing, while Peeta and Annie protest the Games and help her to dream of a world without killing.

Jung believed dreams could restore psychological balance by helping to compensate for people's losses. Most of Katniss's dreams are nightmares of guilt – those she's killed, those she's let die. These are a way of working out her trauma. As she and Peeta relive the Games night after night, they're seeking to find closure, to deal with the terror they faced and find a way through it. Only in her dreams can Katniss allow herself to grieve and rage for the deaths, to hope for a better future. Only through facing what she's given up and bringing it into her everyday life can Katniss find wholeness and healing.

The shadow takes on power in the unconscious world, source of dreams, fantasies, and imaginings. Symbolically, Katniss travels from her ordinary world of surface politeness into the treacherous fantasyland of the Games and her personal magical world, the forest. In both these places, she discovers the bad girl self bubbling beneath the surface and through confronting it, finally develops a kind of stability.

Do What You're Told

Nice girls don't sing creepy songs about hanging trees. They don't complain about the government. Mrs. Everdeen's rules for Katniss's behavior grow positively stifling as she tries to keep Katniss safe in their dystopia. Prim follows the rules every time. She milks her goat and makes cheese – both legal. In *Catching Fire,* she excels in indoor girlish pastimes from flute playing to cooking, all Capitol-approved talents Katniss can't manage. Even when her father dies, Prim can be found sitting neatly at her desk, hands folded, following the rules. Her very nickname, Prim, suggests proper behavior, as does the name of her goat, Lady.

Katniss, the firstborn, has a more difficult burden. She must care for her family and protect them from her mother's despair, the Capitol's oppression, their own starvation. "She has no 'legal' recourse to stop the downward spiral of their existence. All she has are the forbidden hunting skills her father taught her" (Rees 44). For these, she can be executed. The terrible unfairness weighs on her: If she complains and asks for help, she and Prim will have an even worse life.

In many ways, Buttercup is like Katniss's repressed, angry shadow brought to life. She begins the story hating him – he's ugly and useless. But at the same time, he cares for Prim more than anything, like Katniss's inner rage that's determined to protect her childish innocence. He is the savage part of the self, the self that mustn't be allowed out. At the same time, he's part of Katniss, whether she's called Kat-niss or Catnip. As she follows the rules in District Twelve and doesn't voice her anger, even at home, Buttercup hisses and spits like a fire ready to blaze.

> Keenly aware of the long arm of the Capitol, never knowing who is listening to what she, or Prim, or Gale might say in an unguarded moment, Katniss harbors a deep anger and resentment toward the Capitol. The very existence of the reaping further fuels the fire in her belly. But it is a fire she has learned to keep hidden. (Rees 46)

Katniss's only outlet of course is the forest. There she can be a powerful huntress, able to feed her family with a single bowshot. There she and Gale can tease each other and dream of running away. Under the trees, she feels a connection to her father but also to her true self, the side of her that can smile. Her talents are awaiting an outlet.

Being chosen in the reaping is a traumatic moment for Katniss, but deep down it's something of a relief. Fighting for her life in the arena, she won't have to hide. Everything – the archery, the survival skills, the anger and determination can come out at last. The awful responsibility of keeping her family alive is gone – passed to her mother and Gale. As Haymitch points out, there's nothing worse the Capitol can do to her. At last, she can be herself, the independent huntress.

For the first time, too, Katniss is fussed over with sparkling gowns, expensive food, personal trainers, her own stylist and beauty team. For the first time, she's encouraged to tell the world about herself and her dreams. However, she comes out stiff and sullen on camera. In fact, she's spent so much time defensively hiding that she's can't express who she is. The part of her that wants to be pretty and pampered has been burned away by District Twelve, a place where she can't want anything for herself – all the pampering must go to her sister. A place where she's never allowed to have a frosted cake and can only dress up on Reaping Day, the most evil time of all. Offered luxury at last, she's revolted, retreating deep within herself. A good provider, a good District Twelve citizen only survives by not standing out, not hoping or wanting. So she doesn't.

> Underlying Katniss's unacknowledged mixed feelings is the trilogy's own profound ambivalence about desire and power. In some ways, Katniss is more passive than Bella, allowed to have all kinds of goodies but only if she demonstrates her virtue by not really wanting them in the first place.…If Katniss sought to be the center of attention, if she chose to string along two handsome young men more than willing

> to give their lives for hers, if she wanted to have her every movement photographed and admired, if she dreamed of leading the revolution, if she longed to compete and to win – if she had any ambition at all – she would be a bad girl by such a standard. (Miller)

Nice girls aren't greedy or ferocious. Thus, all that happens to Katniss in the Capitol, from the violence of the Games to the luxurious beauty treatments is forced on her. Like Dorothy Gale, "She's not after wealth or fame – she just wants to get home" (Egan 6). Thus she attempts to refuse it all. On Caesar Flickerman's show, Katniss must perform femininity – act sweet and charming to please others, in a parody of her real desires. The audience demands "a hybrid of survivor and show-woman, who can slit a man's throat one moment and giggle and blush like a decorous female the next" (DeaVault 194). This feminine persona is utterly fake for Katniss, designed by Cinna and Haymitch so she can charm the crowds. After so long forbidden to show her anger, her power, her strength, she freezes.

In the film, she's terrified. Her naive, blurted statements ("I was just hoping that I wouldn't burn to death") have the audience laughing at her clear lack of sophistication – they want a confused, awed child, and they're happy to have found one. Peeta's surprise at the showers and Caesar's laughing condescension is similar – good children are not slick – they're lost in the woods. Katniss soon smiles coyly and wins over the audience, but with Cinna's script, Cinna's flaming gown, and only after his nod of approval. Before her few minutes have passed, she's become warm and approachable. But it's Cinna's borrowed charm, not hers.

Though proper girls aren't supposed to become self-important or egotistical, they are supposed to make themselves look beautiful and seek physical admiration. But by trying to perform traditional femininity, Katniss feels more lost and powerless than ever. Katniss can only get sponsors by being a good girl; she can only win the Games by being a bad girl. In training, she snaps and shoots the Gamemakers and is, surprisingly, rewarded for her genuine fierceness with an eleven. She's being offered a path to survival – letting out her rage.

In the Game, Katniss is split once more. Though she longs to help the other children, she knows any sign of weakness might kill her. Rue, sweet and feminine, a gatherer and healer rather than a fighter, is speared like a baby bird and killed by a savage boy. Rue is Katniss's innocent side, the tiny child who, like Prim, must be protected at all costs. Katniss kills her killer, a tough gesture of revenge and rage, but this is not enough of an outlet. Instead, she sings to Rue, allowing out the personal self she always suppresses, and drapes Rue in flowers. Like shooting the Gamemakers' apple, this is Katniss snapping, reminding everyone she's more than their demure, obedient pawn.

Only by following Peeta's advice to be more than a pawn and by singing as Rue begs can Katniss cling to a touch of gentleness in a world that demands savagery. That night, her mind is split into innocent and killer: Katniss can't stop churning with guilt over killing the boy, but she also dreams of Rue singing to the mockingjays, an image of hope and rebellion.

Romance

Katniss appears completely unprepared for romance or sexuality. Miller notes that Katniss

> is unstirred by adolescent hormones, despite the two cute, sweet guys who proclaim their love for her. She may be enmeshed in the kind of romantic triangle that leads fans to don Team This Guy or Team That Guy T-shirts, but the boys' attentions mostly make her unhappy.

Katniss manages to be friendly, even impressive and dazzling in her fiery costumes, but she is hardly an image of seduction. In one telling moment, Peeta calls her too "pure" (*CF* 216) when the other tributes' innuendos embarrass her. Haymitch applauds Peeta's declaration of love, since it's the only thing in his mind that makes asexual Katniss seem "appealing."

In the cave, the downpour strips Katniss of her illegal hunting skills and forces her into the classically good girl roles of romantic heroine and caregiver. She feels inadequate at both, wishing her more feminine mother or Prim were there to help. In the cave, Katniss draws on the memory of her mother, imitating her feminine role model for likely the first time in years. This is a performance: every moment she's aware of the cameras, of the artificial rain the Gamemakers have created like a stage to keep her in place. She acts as she's supposed to and gives her viewers their romance.

Afterward, Katniss takes the role of helpless lovestruck female one step further, conforming to audience expectations and even pushing their sympathy into outrage. "She manipulates the image of the thwarted lovers, pitting the audience's voyeuristic thirst for a televised romantic climax against the Capitol's need to assert dominion" (DeaVault 196). She is expected to be the lovestruck girl: very well then, watch her overplay the part until she offers to kill herself. At the same time, playing this part so fiercely leaves her uncertain of her own feelings and even later she cannot decide whether she was being sincere. Putting on the feminine persona of star-crossed lover has left her more lost than ever.

When Katniss settles into her technology-filled Victor's Village house, she and Buttercup both return to their former home, more comfortable there with the honest squalor and preserved hunting jacket. Like her cat, Katniss hates her new role as figure of admiration and wealth. As she embarks on her Victory Tour in beautiful gowns, flirting publicly with Peeta and enjoying gifts and speeches, she finds she can't connect with genuine emotions. Standing before Thresh and Rue's families, she's barely able to say a word, hidden as she is under the sparkles and spotlights. As the terrible image of an old man being killed for his defiance echoes through her head, Cinna dresses her in a sweetly pink gown and reminds her she must smile for the cameras. Estés explains:

> The problem with "being good" is that it does not resolve the underlying shadow issue, and again, it will rise like a tsunami, like a giant tidal wave, and rush down, destroying everything in its path. In "being good," a woman closes her eyes to everything obdurate, distorted, or damaging around her and just tries to "live with it." (243)

Doing so, however, makes her less likely to change the system. She must lash out.

In her district, Katniss runs away to the woods and the snow, choked as she feels. Her wedding dresses, images of obedience and proper marriage, are the worst. Not only does she run into the forest illegally, but she dreams of running that night, mud streaked, with her wedding gown ripped away by thorns until the real her is revealed.

Everything changes when Snow reveals that her lovestruck act hasn't worked. To her surprise, Katniss feels relief that she can stop pretending. After the Victory Banquet in the Capitol, Katniss dreams Rue visits her as a mockingjay and leads her through the woods. Following her, Katniss feels safe, as though she's found a sanctuary. The time has come for her to retreat to the forest, to stop following the rules and sing in freedom. Before she can run away, however, Katniss is hurled into the Quarter Quell.

In her second tribute parade she is not smiling but angry, not just beautiful but "dark and powerful." Katniss adds, "I love it. Getting to be myself at last" (*CF* 212). As Cinna points out, her days of childish pink lipstick and hair ribbons are gone. She no longer pretends for Caesar's audience, but proudly acknowledges the victor she's become. In the Games, Katniss fantasizes about killing Snow and stops herself. "Not very pretty daydreams for a seventeen-year-old girl, I guess," she thinks uncomfortably (*CF* 329). Like her smoking wedding gown, the good girl mask is crumbling away.

In the Quell, she makes herself a warrior woman determined to protect Peeta, even at the cost of her life. However she is overcome with shock when she discovers her true helplessness: she has been a pawn, with every tribute conspiring to save her and make her their figurehead. All the time, Katniss has been useless, ignorant of the escape plan and trapped in the Games while Peeta is captured and her own district bombed into nothing. After this, she withdraws into nightmares and despair, unable to function.

Echoes of the Self

Katniss's dilemma becomes even clearer in *Mockingjay*, as she's sandwiched between contrasts. Annie is the traumatized good girl, Johanna the traumatized bad girl. Hurt and lost as Katniss is, she must decide which she wants to be, while both tug at her like an angel and devil on her shoulders.

Annie means grace or favor, but her "favored" status comes from her loved ones. She is not a savior of others – she's the one heroes like Mags and Finnick die to protect. As such, she's another Prim, fragile and childlike. Even her name is babyish. She is also the star-crossed lover Katniss only pretends to be – Annie and Finnick truly adore each other but are kept apart as Snow uses Finnick and threatens Annie as a hostage. They were both chosen for the Quarter Quell (in a doubtless prearranged moment), and Snow might have tried forcing one to kill the other had Mags not taken Annie's place. Finnick and Annie's doomed, short-lived romance is all Katniss and Peeta pretend to have on camera, from their reunion, to wedding, to baby, to Finnick's tragic sacrifice.

The name Johanna means "grace of God" and so is deeply related to Annie's name. It also hints at independence – Johanna may have luck, but she lacks earthly protection of family and friends. She and Annie are polar opposites: She is argumentative, sarcastic, unwilling to censor her rudeness. Annie, who is kept less informed than Katniss, has only five lines in the series. Johanna comes from the forest, Annie from the oceanside. Annie is classically feminine but Johanna uses her sexuality to keep people off-balance, stripping in front of Katniss to make her blush. She wrestles and swings a woodcutter's axe, traditional male skills. Further, in her childhood Game, Johanna deceived the others and made herself *look* weak and then savagely murdered other tributes. Annie won her Game simply by surviving – swimming better than all the others. As Katniss looks on Annie as a needy younger sister, she comments, watching Johanna, "I wonder if this is what it's like to have an older sister who really hates you" (*CF* 324).

In District Thirteen, Katniss witnesses Finnick and Annie's immense love, so great that only being together is all they need. But Johanna, memorably comments, "They can't hurt me. I'm not like the rest of you. There's no one left I love" (*CF* 347). Seeing her, Katniss is warned of whom she will become if she rejects Peeta and her family, walls herself off from emotion so she won't get hurt. Johanna is not as healthy as she appears.

> When Peeta and Katniss are each wounded, just as deeply as Johanna, they have each other there to help them on the slow and rocky path to recovery. Johanna is no less damaged for her lack of love, but she doesn't have anyone to help her back afterwards. (Borsellino 38)

Annie and Finnick, by contrast, want to marry and have children, even in the midst of death and war.

"People who passionately irk us are usually mirroring our own shadows back to us, though ours may surface with a different rendition that we do not recognize" (Badonsky). Here is Johanna, who so annoys Katniss because she's like the bad girl voice within her, eager for revenge against the Capitol, defensive and isolated. Johanna's crippling injuries, addiction to painkillers, and lack of possessions all mirror Katniss's problems, pushed to an extreme. She says all Katniss has been holding back – Katniss is positively stunned when Johanna yells, "Whole country in rebellion? Wouldn't want anything like that," as a threat to the Gamemakers, right in the middle of the Game (*CF* 346). All her friends are hinting at such a thing. But to say it aloud? Katniss half-expects lightning to strike Johanna on the spot.

Johanna and Katniss snarl at each other (and swear and pinch in Johanna's case), but Johanna is frequently right: Katniss feels good after she dances at Annie's wedding where Snow can see her. Johanna talks openly about her torture and nightmares, encouraging Katniss to do likewise. Only Johanna dragging her from bed helps her get through her pain and start training. Johanna even makes her move out of the hospital, and in with her. After discovering how Peeta's been hijacked "everything screams" in Katniss's dreams (*MJ* 245). But Johanna tries to help her sort through it and channel her pain into revenge. Though they joke about killing each other, they each become sources of strength in the other's lives. A good girl cannot handle the pain, but a bad one can.

"Oh, the energy we use in this society to suppress what we perceive to be our undesirable traits – our negativity, judgmental nature, and our other secret peculiarities and struggles" (Badonsky). Well-behaved citizens try to be kind and sweet like Annie, but it is the negativity and pain that often lead to greatness. Katniss's rage at Snow forces her to run each day with Johanna, train, and become a soldier. The shadow is a voice of repressed desires, but a source of rage and inner fire when one learns to listen.

At story's end, Johanna votes to continue the Games to punish other children as she has been. Annie votes no, determined to protect the innocent. As they provide examples for Katniss, she witnesses two kinds of strength – Johanna has physical power that helps her shake off a morphling addiction but betrays her when she's traumatized in training. Annie has emotional strength that lets her survive the Capitol's torture to see Finnick again and let herself wed him. From this lesson, Katniss learns that loving and traditional feminine abilities aren't weakness – they can be a source of enormous power. She follows Annie's example by the book's end. When she manages to trust, marry, and even have children, she becomes a heroine Prim and Rue would admire.

Lashing Out

After her District is bombed, Katniss visits, silent and sorrowing, and returns with only Buttercup. With her rage symbolically returned to her, she agrees to become the Mockingjay and comes out of her isolation. In the District Thirteen bombing, Katniss has her most direct moment of identification with the cat:

> Crazy Cat becomes a metaphor for my situation. I am Buttercup. Peeta, the thing I want so badly to secure, is the light. As long as Buttercup feels he has the chance of catching the elusive light under his paws, he's bristling with aggression… (*MJ* 153).

Watching the repressed inner rage inside her go crazy, batting at the dancing light, Katniss realizes what she has become and why she's so helpless to succeed. Whatever she does, Peeta will pay the price. There, in the darkest basement of District Thirteen and of her soul, she spends the rest of that night close to her shadow, "obsessively making knots, holding them up for Buttercup's inspection" (*MJ* 156). She cannot simply retreat inside herself – instead she harnesses the strength she sees in her cat and goes into battle.

On the higher, public levels of District Thirteen, every moment of Katniss's day is scheduled and every bite has been weighed for optimum calories. In the midst of this, Katniss has suppressed all desires so she can fit into the collective society. When asked what she'd like for herself, she can't even answer. Then, without volition, her hand writes "*I KILL SNOW*" (*MJ* 38, caps and italics in orig.). This is the shadow, the repressed personality bursting forth to speak.

"When a woman agrees to become too 'well-bred' her instincts for these [wild] impulses drop down into her darkest unconscious, outside her automatic reach" (Estés 233). She finds herself unable to summon passion, ferocity, or anger, instead appearing numb or withdrawn. Here is Katniss at the close of *Mockingjay*. She has obeyed her superiors, suppressed her fears and desires to become a good soldier, refused power and rejected greed, and as a result, she has lost the one person she valued over all others. While she might have survived the deaths of Peeta or Gale, Prim represents her precious vulnerability.

With this shock, Katniss becomes so deadened that she loses the ability to speak. In her dreams, Delly, another good girl, is "prattling on about the niceness of people" (*MJ* 350). Beside her are Mr. Everdeen and Cinna, and all the dead of the series. The good ones fly above Katniss like birds, the bad ones try to drag her under the sea. Her dream is warning her that she can fly and sing, regrow her feathers and be a symbol of life once more. Or she can sink into apathy and die. The presence of Delly versus Mr. Everdeen, the nice obedient girl versus the rebel who taught Katniss to sing and hunt, reflects her struggle. Beside them, Cinna stitches a new wedding dress. He has been the only one in the series to let Katniss choose, to insist Katniss should only be the Mockingjay if she wishes. This offer of a wedding dress seems like another choice, waiting for Katniss should she want to accept.

In time, Katniss regains a modicum of her nice-girl persona, dresses carefully, attends Coin's meetings. She votes to hold a last Game, since that is what Coin expects from her. And then, as with the book's beginning, Katniss's starving shadow takes control. Possibly even without her conscious choice, she kills Coin.

> In the view of analytical psychology, the repression of both negative and positive instincts, urges, and feelings into the unconscious causes them to inhabit a shadow realm. While the ego and superego [or rational mind] attempt to continue to censor the shadow impulses, the very pressure that repression causes is rather like a bubble in the sidewall of a tire. Eventually, as the tire revolves and heats up, the pressure behind the bubble intensifies, causing it to explode outward, releasing all the inner content. (Estés 236)

Like her hand writing her need for vengeance, for an end to tyranny, Katniss's bow arm shoots the real culprit, the real murderess of sweet Prim. Like her shot at the Gamemakers' apple, like her runs into the forest, Katniss has simply snapped. Culturally, ladies aren't supposed to get angry, mustn't yell or lash out. But Katniss has had enough of proper behavior.

After she shoots Coin, Katniss is stripped of everything, even her newly healing skin. Bleeding and hopeless, she curls up in a bed exposed down to the mattress with a gaping, empty closet beside her, "feeling so naked with just the paper to cover my tender flesh," as she says (*MJ* 375).

Nice girls are quiet: they don't speak up for themselves, sing subversive songs, or make a fuss. They don't kill the enemy; they die trapped like Rue or helping others like Prim. They are mild, kind, and above all meek.

> Fairytales show silent, virtuous maids like Cinderella and the little mermaid, who never complain of their vicious treatment, and even more silent, virtuous but dead mothers. Contrasted with this are the vocal witches and stepmothers giving orders. (Frankel, *From Girl to Goddess* 22)

The message is clear: be passive, do whatever the tyrant orders, nod and smile, and perhaps survive. Those who disobey become Avoxes or worse.

In fact, the series is filled with voiceless victims, beginning with the withdrawn Mrs. Everdeen and Lavinia the Avox. Following her are the inarticulate Mags and Wiress, the silent morphling woman who dies for Peeta, and all the other dead tributes. Annie, too traumatized to communicate rationally. Octavia and Venia, confined in a cell. Most of all are the dead: innocent Rue and Prim, sweet, quiet Madge, the voiceless nameless children sacrificed in so many games. Katniss also learns of gentle Maysilee Donner and her bedridden twin, from whom she inherited the mockingjay pin. All of these offer silent pleas to end the fighting, for they can no longer speak for themselves.

"Silenced women in myth echo silenced women in today's world, illiterate and confined to cleaning and childbearing" (Frankel, *From Girl to Goddess* 21). Too many people today, especially women, are unable to vote, unable to let their voices past the censors. The many silenced women of the series mirror this repression, until Katniss finally finds a way to share their sorrows in her book.

Katniss herself becomes a "mental Avox" after she snaps. Only after the creative, furious shadow has escaped, can traumatized Katniss find wholeness and healing. To her surprise, she begins to sing. "Hour after hour of ballads, love songs, mountain airs. All the songs my father taught me before he died, for certainly there has been very little music in my life since" (*MJ* 376). When she's in the hospital, badly burned, she dreams of her father singing her "The Hanging Tree" and warning her to keep it secret. Dreams are the shadow's way of crying for attention, of reminding the conscious self what she isn't dealing with. Her singing demands a voice.

It's the voice of grief and loss but also the voice of freedom, for a girl who has been repressed too long. Estés notes:

> When the treasure of a woman's most soulful life has been burned to ashes, instead of being driven by anticipation, a woman is possessed by voraciousness. So, for instance, if a woman wasn't permitted to sculpt, she may suddenly begin to sculpt day and night. (230)

In her article "The Shadow Muse – Gifts of Your Dark Side," Jill Badonsky notes that the emotions of our shadow side provide "an incredible amount of creative energy. Anger, jealousy, revenge, frustration, sadness, rejection have been conduits for so many triumphant works of writing, art, music and performance." It's not surprising that "good girl" Katniss doesn't sing – this is a tool only available to subversive Katniss by the lake. As Katniss sings even in her Capitol prison, she reconnects with this lost side of herself and struggles toward wholeness.

Before the Games, Peeta only paints little flowers on cakes. Afterwards, his paintings have reached a new level of expression, as he recreates his dark nightmares through art instead of dreams. This makes him "a little less afraid of going to sleep at night" (*CF* 54). His painting has become the Games, a memorial but also a cry for the savagery to end. In particular, he paints Rue to hold the Capitol responsible for her murder. "It's better for me to wake up with a paintbrush than a knife in my hand," he admits (*CF* 54). On sight Katniss hates them but must admit they're "extraordinary."

> The energy of anger and envy can also fuel constructive action and motivation. The fine line between madness and creativity attests to how our dark individuality can be exalted by giving it a creative expression. (Badonsky)

Torn by insanity later, Peeta uses art as therapy, decorating Annie's wedding cake with symbols of the nurturing ocean. In the end, as he and Katniss struggle to heal, he continues painting as well as baking. Beside him, Katniss writes, and she and Haymitch at last find an outlet for their sorrows.

Finding Balance

Returning to District Twelve, Katniss finds all is different. Her hunting is sanctioned, as Greasy Sae encourages her to go out and the townsfolk give her a cart ride. Her father's bow, no longer hidden in the forest, is waiting in her house. And her relationship with Peeta, always a public spectacle for the camera, is now private and quiet, her choice at last rather than the Capitol's.

Buttercup arrives, and, after screaming at the neglected, miserable cat, Katniss finds a way to love and forgive him, and thus love and forgive the neglected, miserable side of herself.

> At this point, Katniss and Buttercup both break down with grief over the loss of Prim. They reconcile with each other and Buttercup begins guarding Katniss just as he guarded Prim. Based on comments about the book, many people found this point to be the emotional peak of the series. In addition, I think it represents the key turning point in Katniss's relationship with herself. After this she is willing to love Peeta. She no longer blames herself for all the problems of the world. In the epilogue Buttercup is no longer present. I think this is a sign that Katniss is now one with herself. She no longer needs an alter ego. (Barkmeier)

By reconciling with her shadow, she finds a kind of peace.

In fact, Katniss finds a secure balance at last, loving and hunting as she works through her long silence to sing once more. In District Twelve she is no longer forbidden to be herself. The fence between meadow and town has come down, like the split in her heart. Together with Peeta, she begins her great project, a memorial book. As she sings and writes, hunts in the forest and lives in town, she's found a way to welcome the creative shadow.

KATNISS THE CHOSEN ONE AND THESEUS THE HERO

Suzanne Collins explains in several interviews that the Games themselves were inspired by the classical myth of Theseus. Every nine years, seven Athenian boys and seven Athenian girls were sent to Crete as tributes and locked in the labyrinth for the bull-headed Minotaur to devour. Collins comments, "My 24 boys and girls who must fight to the death for the entertainment of the Capitol are also called "tributes," like the Athenian youth, and after taking the place of her sister, Prim, who would surely have died, the story's heroine, Katniss, joins the other tributes but is continuously defiant of the Capitol" (Blasingame). One year, the valiant Prince Theseus volunteers. Upon arriving, he navigates the terrible labyrinth of Crete and slays the Minotaur.

In his heroic quest, Theseus follows the same pattern as Harry Potter, Percy Jackson, and many other heroes from myth and literature. Though this pattern of the Chosen One is universal, Joseph Campbell is the famed folklorist who charted the journey step by step in his groundbreaking *The Hero with a Thousand Faces.* As Campbell relates, "The hero feels something's lacking in his life. He then goes off to recover it or to discover a life-giving elixir. There's a cycle of going and returning" (123). The hero typically leaves home with a magic sword and enters the Otherworld. There he descends into the darkest place of all, in this case the labyrinth. At the climax of this quest, the hero confronts the ultimate enemy – a shadow that represents his dark side, his angry and submerged half. He then returns home with new wisdom to share. This classic quest is a metaphor for facing one's dark side, for growing from child to adult and becoming a leader for the next generation.

Though it's less known, the classic heroine too has a journey, found in ancient epics across the world, as well as fairytales and modern fantasy novels. Her goal is to become the all-powerful mother. Thus, many heroines set out on missions to rescue their shattered families: Meg Murray of *A Wrinkle in Time* quests to save her father then her little brother. Coraline tries to save her parents, Meggie of *Inkheart* and Clary of *The Mortal Instruments,* their mothers. Tim Burton's Alice tries to rescue the Mad Hatter. Scores of young women in folklore rescue their lovers from fairies, demons, and ogres. Demeter forces herself into the realm of the dead to reclaim her daughter, while Isis scours the world for her husband's broken body. Katniss, of course, spends the series protecting Prim and her growing adoptive family, from Peeta to the children of Panem. Gary Ross comments:

> One of the things that's made the books so popular is that Katniss struggles for and maintains her own humanity in the face of a culture that wants to take it from her. By the end [of book one], she's willing to die rather than take an innocent life. She's a phenomenal hero, and I think that's very inspiring and redemptive. ("Prattle Royale")

Though the goal is rescuing beloved family members or potential husbands, these heroines work as hard as any fairytale heroes. Looking at these two patterns side by side will show similarities and differences between the two models of quest.

Campbell's Hero's Journey	**Theseus**	***The Hunger Games***	**The Heroine's Journey**
The World of Common Day	Theseus grows up in the countryside.	Katniss grows up in District Twelve	The World of Common Day
The Call To Adventure	Theseus claims his father's sword.	Prim is chosen in the reaping, so Katniss volunteers instead.	The Call To Adventure
Refusal of the Call	He doesn't want to go.	She doesn't want to go.	Refusal of the Call
Supernatural Aid	Charon tutors him in war and heroics.	Haymitch offers advice and sponsor gifts, Cinna makes beautiful gowns.	The Warrior's Male Mentors

Campbell	Theseus	*The Hunger Games*	**Heroine Journey**
Supernatural Aid	The king's sword	Her father's bow, her father's book	Bladeless Talisman
The Crossing of the First Threshold	Theseus journeys to Athens, then Crete.	Katniss journeys to the exotic Capitol	The Crossing of the First Threshold
Innermost Cave	He enters the Labyrinth.	Katniss enters the Games, the Quarter Quell, then the battle in the Capitol	Opening One's Senses
The Road of Trials	With his fellow tributes, Theseus navigates the Labyrinth.	She's helped by Rue, Peeta, and Thresh; her Quarter Quell allies; and her Star Squad.	Sidekicks, Trials, Adversaries
The Meeting With the Goddess	Ariadne guides him with her magic thread and they fall in love.	Katniss comes to care for Peeta, her gentle sensitive side.	Finding the Sensitive Man
		Katniss sees Haymitch betray her and meets deposed Snow. She reconciles with each.	Confronting the Powerless Father

Campbell	Theseus	*The Hunger Games*	Heroine Journey
Atonement with the Father	Theseus battles the Minotaur.	Katniss understands who Coin is and says what she wants to hear.	Atonement with the Mother
Apotheosis	Theseus succeeds and wins the gods' favor.	Katniss dreams she is a phoenix, rising from her own ashes.	Integration and Apotheosis
The Ultimate Boon	Theseus escapes with Ariadne – the tribute has ended forever.	To protect the children of Panem, Katniss shoots Coin.	Reward: Winning the Family
Refusal of the Return	Theseus is uncertain what awaits him.	Katniss wants to kill herself, but finally manages to heal.	Torn Desires
The Crossing of the Return Threshold	Theseus returns to Athens and is crowned.	Back in District Twelve Katniss builds a new family with Peeta and Haymitch.	Return
Master of the Two Worlds	Theseus is now king – he has grown from child to adult.	She returns to hunting, marries and accepts the risk of children.	Power over Life and Death

A New World

"In the first stage of this kind of adventure, the hero leaves the realm of the familiar, over which he has some measure of control, and comes to a threshold" (Campbell 146). For Theseus, this is the start of his grand exploits. For Katniss, it's her journey from District Twelve to the Capitol. As with *Harry Potter, Star Wars,* and other series, Katniss's first book is a perfect Chosen One pattern, as is the arc of the entire series.

The heroic child grows up in obscurity, raised by foster parents and ignorant of his true origin. Theseus, like many Greek heroes, trains with the centaur Chiron and becomes a warrior. When he reaches maturity at age sixteen, Theseus' mother Aethra tells him that he's the son of Aegeus, king of Athens, or so it's thought – his real father is actually the god of the sea, Poseidon. Theseus lifts a giant rock and finds beneath it the king's sword and sandals. With them, he takes the dangerous overland route to Athens to meet the king. On the way he encounters a long list of robbers and monsters: Periphetes, Sinis, Phaea the Cromyonian sow, Sciron, Cercyon, and Procrustes. He's small for a warrior, but he defeats them all by using their own strength against them. At Athens, Theseus is welcomed by Aegeus, who crowns him as his son and heir.

Katniss's early battles are not with monsters, but with the starvation and deprivation inflicted by the Capitol. Her first priority is to protect and feed her sister, the only person she truly loves. "This is actually a girl whose fierceness comes from a nurturing place, not a conquering place," comments producer Nina Jacobson (Egan 22). This is the heroine's journey: protection and salvation rather than conquest. At the same time, she's gaining a warrior's skills. Her father is dead and her mother, too withdrawn to care for her. Thus Katniss, like Theseus, gains a heroic independence early on.

Theseus has his father's sword, a classic tool for heroes from King Arthur to Luke Skywalker. More common for heroines are tools of wisdom like a golden compass or like Coraline's round stone, which reveals her the truth around her when she gazes through its opening. Magic mirrors and spyglasses heighten the heroine's perception. Books are even more popular as tools of wisdom, appearing in *Inkheart, Ella Enchanted, The Spiderwick Chronicles, The Mortal Instruments, The Kane Chronicles,* and *A Series of Unfortunate Events.* Katniss of course has her father's precious logbook, with descriptions of edible plants.

> It contains a guide of all his knowledge, his incredible forest lore that saves her family from starvation and then helps her survive in the Games. Katniss calls it "the place where we recorded those things you cannot trust to memory," as the notes reveal which similar-looking plants can kill and which heal (*MJ* 387). Of course, the book's other great power is that it can be passed on to posterity. As the series continues, she

> keeps the book and his hunting jacket close like talismans to protect her against the world's evils.
>
> While Katniss and Peeta add to the book in *Catching Fire*, the logbook foreshadows her final book, written as a tribute to the Games and the war that follows. All of her precious memories are recorded there, and not just to immortalize her loved ones. This is also a book with things too precious to be trusted to memory: the message that war destroys the innocent and causes suffering that must not come again. She can pass it on to her children and use it to "make them braver" (*MJ* 390) and guide them toward a future in which humanity can outgrow war. (Frankel, *Katniss* 71-72)

The heroine generally wields a distance weapon, like wind and water magic or moon arrows. Katniss's bow casts her as Artemis, the huntress. It's a link with the natural world and also her source of power. In the Games, Katniss uses her bow to trip the mines surrounding the Careers' supplies, and to slay the unholy mutts that the Capitol sends. She also shoots the final tribute in a gesture of compassion, a mercy killing.

In Greek myth, Theseus's father King Aegeus once had held a great set of games, in which Minos's son Androgeus was killed by a bull. Minos declared war on Athens and prayed for vengeance from the gods. Famine and plague devastated Athens, until Aegeus offered Minos whatever he wished. Minos ordered him to send seven youths and seven maidens each decade to be fodder for the Minotaur. Like Coin at the series end, Minos craves revenge, not justice. His son has died, so dozens of children must die in return. Theseus, like Katniss, is appalled at this cruelty.

Soon enough, Katniss and Theseus each volunteer for the tribute. (Sources vary on this: most say Theseus volunteers, but one has the lot falling on him by chance and one has Minos selecting the victims for himself. This last of course echoes Snow's hand-selecting victors in the second Games). Katniss wants only to save her sister, while Theseus hopes to break the strength of their oppressor, slaying the Minotaur and ending the Tribute forever.

The Minoan civilization was ancient and powerful, with the palace at Knossos a grandiose fortress of the Bronze Age. Women wore tiered skirts and revealing open jackets far removed from the undyed Greek tunics. They traded in exotic Egyptian delicacies and perfumes. Knossos itself was an intricate maze of 1300 interlocking rooms, with artisans' workrooms and wine presses around a central square decorated with extensive frescoes. With an aqueduct system and even the first flushing toilet, this palace was a marvel of ancient technology. Upon entering it, Theseus and his friends must have felt uncultured barbarians indeed.

Katniss too is amazed by running water, exotic foods, and colorful fashions as she enters the Capitol. When tributes like Johanna and Finnick strip, she feels terribly embarrassed and provincial. There's technology and luxury beyond anything she's seen, from chocolate fondue to shower massages. But all this is preparation for the dark cave in which she must confront her darkest fears: The Games themselves.

Innermost Cave

After traveling to this foreign land of near-magical technology, Katniss and Theseus both enter the true arena. For Katniss, this is the artificial world of the Game itself, a bubble of traps and constructed dangers. She endures the Games in each book, with the war in the Capitol itself as the third, deadliest Game. For Theseus, it is the labyrinth, a magical maze under the palace "from which there was no escape after one entered, for it closed off its imperceivable exit with convoluted flexions [joints]." (Apollodorus 3.213). It, like the Games, is a sealed environment, an underworld where Theseus is condemned to die. He must kill the Minotaur trapped inside, or it will kill him.

Campbell explains that in classic tales, "the hero is swallowed and taken into the abyss to be later resurrected – a variant of the death-and-resurrection theme" (146). Harry Potter takes the Hogwarts Express to the magical realm of Hogwarts, and then descends into the dungeons or the graveyard to pass his great test. In the Innermost Cave, the hero often dies (as Harry does) only to return once more. This is a metaphor for going through a crisis and emerging stronger, armed with the wisdom of adulthood.

In many fairytales from Andersen's "The Little Mermaid" to "The Six Swans," the heroine's most dire struggle takes place high in the prince's castle, far from her magical forest or ocean. This is the world of order and tyranny, where the young heroine is truly helpless. The Games are a similar trap, where the Gamemakers can torture Katniss with mutts and arbitrary rules. Though she knows how to protect and feed herself in the trees, she's helpless when the woods explode in fire, or endless rain scares off the animals. Jabberjays afflict her in the middle of the Quarter Quell, shrieking in Prim's voice. Monkeys attack and rain burns like poison. All the symbols of nature, the feminine world, have been twisted by Capitol technology. This is a place of trial, an ordeal that burns Katniss down to her strongest inner core.

At the climax of the Innermost Cave, the questing heroine often falls into a magic sleep, like Snow White or Sleeping Beauty withdrawn from the world. This marks a cocoon-like transformation between one stage of being and another – frequently childhood and adulthood.

> Snow White lies unconscious, perfectly preserved in glass, but at the same time, the coffin is like a crucible, transforming her from frightened child into powerful queen. This sleep, of course, symbolizes the heroine's descent into death, where she must confront her mortality and gain wisdom from the experience. When she wakes, she has become stronger. (Frankel, *From Girl to Goddess* 30).

Katniss has several descents into deathlike sleep. Her madness and drug-induced hospitalization at the end of each book signals a journey into the unconscious world of dreams and visions. Lying there, Katniss must confront the terrors and guilt of her actions and battle through them to accept whom she's become. Only afterward can she put all the deaths and losses into perspective. After Katniss's terrible burning in *Mockingjay*, she is locked away, unseen by the world, unable to speak. She sinks into delirious dreams that resemble a journey into the underworld as she sees her loved ones from Cinna to her father. She herself is a fiery bird drowning in the sea, but she awakes with new skin, risen from her own ashes like a phoenix.

Her most literal and bravest brush with death comes at the end of *The Hunger Games* when she lifts a nightlock berry to her lips, "taking one last look at the world (*HG* 345). Though the suicide is meant as a subterfuge, Katniss knows that if the Gamemakers don't relent, she and Peeta will both die there in the arena. She comes through her ordeal with the shining knowledge that the Capitol can be outwitted, even beaten.

THE GUIDE

Campbell describes the need for those trapped in the labyrinth to have a guide who represents the heart, a conscience to point the way. Theseus only escapes the maze with the wisdom and compassion of Ariadne, King Minos's daughter. Her name means "very holy one," casting her as a sacred guide in the story (Walker 158). Out of love, she gives him a magic ball of thread to guide him through the labyrinth, without which he would surely have perished.

Thus the hero's guardian protects him like a kindly mother as she shows him how to tap the buried feminine within himself. Harry Potter sees his mother, Lily, in mirrors, photographs, and memories locked in a swirling pensieve, and then finally summons her with his resurrection stone in the final book. "Stay with me," he tells her as he descends into the dark forest to die, and her presence banishes the terrible dementors. Galadriel tests Frodo's heart with her magic mirror, and the Lady of the Lake gives Arthur a scabbard to heal his wounds. Meeting the motherly force of protection is a moment of comforting magic, a time of healing before the dark trials ahead. She is life, the power of creation and emotion itself. Her light is one the hero can summon to shield him from the darkest peril. Meeting her, he gains protection that will aid him in confronting his deadliest adversary – the monster in the heart of the maze.

Katniss the warrior woman has refined her masculine fighting abilities but not her gentler skills. Thus, like the classic hero, she's aided by perceptive, emotional helpers: sweet, tiny Rue and lighthearted, trusting Peeta. Both offer perspectives Katniss lacks. Rue points out the tracker jackers Katniss hasn't spotted, and mentions that Peeta's love doesn't seem to be an act. She knows edible plants and the healing leaves Katniss has mostly forgotten, while Peeta jokes and teases. He makes small luxuries for Katniss, like a plastic raincover or apple slices on toast. Rue is a singer and Peeta a painter, forces of creativity to supplement Katniss's warrior strength. They both keep watch over her while she sleeps. Katniss herself does best with someone to protect, someone to keep her grounded in the world of life and love. More literally, caring for Rue earns her Thresh's help, while protecting Peeta gets her gifts from sponsors: Loving them makes others love her. Without both of them she would not survive.

Campbell notes: "All these different mythologies give us the same essential quest. You leave the world that you're in and go into a depth or into a distance or up to a height. There you come to what was missing in your consciousness" (129). For Katniss this is feminine sensitivity, gentleness, and love. Katniss finds Peeta dying of infection and must face the nurturing side she's never confronted in herself. She coxes, begs, threatens, and kisses Peeta into drinking broth and keeps him alive until she can get the medicine to save him. Her kisses for the camera feel strange as she taps the nurturing feminine side she has never explored in years of hunting. When she kisses him, she takes her first tiny steps into a world of trusting others and being cared for in turn.

The Tyrant

On the heroine's journey, the young questor comes to realize that she is mightier than the tyrant: Dorothy cowers before the "Great and Powerful Oz" when she reaches his Emerald City. But after facing the far more terrifying Wicked Witch of the West, she grows into someone strong enough to kick over the Wizard's pasteboard head and confront the fraud cowering behind it. Katniss too realizes that the Capitol's *threat* far outweighs the Capitol itself. As she declares on one of her broadcasts: "The Capitol's fragile because it depends on the districts for everything. Food, energy, even the Peacekeepers that police us. If we declare our freedom, the Capitol collapses. President Snow, thanks to you, I'm officially declaring mine today" (*MJ* 169). Like their broken electric fences, the Capitol has only the illusion of authority, until Katniss can shatter it. At series end, she meets Snow heavily shackled and helpless in his rose garden and knows she can kill him.

Donald Sutherland (Snow) describes his character, saying:

> I think he sees challenge and I think he sees it in this Katniss Everdeen. I think he sees in her the challenge that he's been waiting for. You know, sitting there, somebody someday is going to come up sometime. And this particular one, given how it's all gone, you can't just kill her. You have to find some other way of controlling her, containing her. (Lesnick)

He fails: Katniss is too strong once she takes charge of her own destiny.

The classic heroine learns independence, not protection from her father-figure. Lyra of *The Golden Compass* discovers that her father is a murderer when he kills her helpless friend Roger. Meg Murray crosses time and space to rescue her blinded and confused father, and they tesseract to a friendly planet. When Meg demands that he return to rescue her brother Charles Wallace, Meg's three witch mentors appear and tell Meg her father is not powerful enough. Meg gazes sadly at him. "I wanted you to do it all for me…I was scared, and I didn't want to have to do anything myself" (L'Engle 187). With this, she acknowledges she is the only one who can rescue Charles Wallace, so she returns to confront the monstrous IT.

Cinna, Boggs, Finnick, and Katniss's father die, Gale is whipped in the square, and then he and Beetee are revealed as accidental masterminds behind Prim's death. Peeta is hijacked. In the course of the series, all the powerful males in Katniss's life, from mentors to friends, lose their power.

Katniss's official mentor, Haymitch, is another example of the flawed masculine authority. In the first book, his sponsor gifts float down like boons from the gods. Haymitch watches over her like a father, offering gifts but also withholding them to show her what she must do, how she must behave to survive. *Catching Fire* is much the same. However, he is revealed as imperfect when he fails to save Peeta. His guardianship, his advice, have all proved useless because he could not protect one vulnerable child from the Capitol. In District Thirteen, Haymitch is wretchedly ill, even laughable, as he "dries out" from his alcoholism. When he reappears, Katniss has lost respect for him.

By realizing that the male authority's power over her has ended, the heroine finds independence and strength. She need not obey his laws, but can make her own wiser ones. "Her own individual morality triggers a revolution – her own ethical line – what she finds out about herself triggers a revolution," Gary Ross notes ("Conversation"). Katniss rejects Haymitch's authority, and after Boggs dies, she leads her own mission to assassinate Snow. She perseveres through Snow's threats and traps, his brainwashing of Peeta and the vicious mutts he sends hunting her through the city, all to see him die in the Capitol square.

The Shadow

At the same time, Snow is not the greatest threat, nor is Minos. Theseus doesn't journey into the labyrinth to confront the king, but the monstrous Minotaur, his own deadly shadow.

The shadow, in psychology, is "aspects of oneself which are considered by the ego to be undesirable or not useful and are therefore relegated to the dark" (Estés 85). Often the hero or heroine meets a monster or person who embodies all the qualities he or she rejects: the ugly, greedy, misbehaving force of destruction. Jung explains that the shadow personifies everything a person refuses to acknowledge about himself and yet is always thrusting itself at him, as a lingering voice of greed or dissatisfaction. Only by facing these unwanted qualities can the hero become wise.

Harry Potter realizes that he could have been Voldemort if he'd made different choices: both are half-blood orphans, both grew up with the Muggles and cling to Hogwarts as a sanctuary. Luke and Darth Vader are even closer, though one fights for good and one for evil. This is the moment of facing the shadow, when Frodo realizes he could easily become the creeping, vicious Gollum.

The Minotaur is a savage, bull-headed man. If Theseus represents the clever side of fighting, the Minotaur is all instinct and brutality. It is gigantic, lumbering, bestial, as Theseus is quick and agile. It is a devourer of innocents, eater of the children Theseus has trained. When Theseus battles it, he is confronting the raging, uncontrolled monster inside himself, learning to master it, and destroying its power over him. With the monster beheaded, Theseus seizes Princess Ariadne and escapes with her back to Athens. Frequently, this is a father-son battle between Luke and Darth or Theseus and the tyrant. By destroying Minos's authority, Theseus symbolically grows past his father's influence and becomes an adult.

For the heroine, the ugly inner voice is the evil witch, murderess of the innocent. This woman is as powerful and tyrannical as the heroine is childish. She is Mrs. Coulter of *The Golden Compass*, who murders children in deadly experiments. The dried up Wicked Witch of the West. Jadis, the White Witch, who freezes Narnia in sterile winter. All the wicked stepmothers and witches from the catalogue of Disney villainesses.

Though Katniss realizes it too late, this adversary is President Coin. Coin tortures Katniss's childlike prep team, and Katniss soon realizes this is meant as a declaration of her authority. When Coin assigns Peeta to Katniss's squad, Katniss knows Coin wants her more than controlled: she wants her dead. Katniss has become so likeable that Coin fears for her own position. "You're the face of the rebellion. You may have more influence than any other single person," Boggs tells her (*MJ* 266). Coin is not a wise leader, but a jealous force of sterility and cruelty – she must control everything, or it must perish.

"The woman who views marriage as a reassignment of living quarters cannot anticipate the steadfast core of Katniss's compassion. She nor Snow ever really understand love at all" (Borsellino 38). Coin has no apparent family, no one she cares to protect. In this, as with everything else, they are opposite extremes. The active, loving, battling Katniss has more power than Coin has ever had, from her hunting skills to her circle of loved ones. Thus Coin, like Snow White's stepmother, resolves to destroy her to maintain her own rulership. Katniss is a beloved symbol of revolution, Katniss could name another to be president; therefore, Katniss must die.

Their conflict is a metaphor for the mother-daughter battle for independence. The daughter is growing up, claiming power in her life as she discovers adulthood. "Mother and daughter start off as a single united set of desires, one that can be challenging for the daughter to reject without rejecting the mother's love, while the mother has an equally hard time accepting the daughter as a distinct individual" (Frankel, *From Girl to Goddess* 133). If the mother is unwilling to give up control and let her daughter become the new heroine and ruler of the world, the two must battle. Here is the tale of Cinderella or Snow White, in which the mother will not give up her role as the fairest to let the girl win her happy ending. Frequently in tales, a wicked stepmother is substituted for the real mother, to soften the pain of the conflict. Coin is the surrogate mother and president of District Thirteen, but not Katniss's relation.

Katniss must realize who her true enemy is. Snow is a murderer of children, but Coin is the one to murder Katniss's sister. Worse yet, Coin's Games will resurrect the cycle of the Games, taking revenge on the innocent. Katniss aims her silver bow at her true target and fires. She makes the decision to kill Coin "to eliminate the threat of violence in the future, rather than take revenge for violence in the past" (Brennan 9). As she did in the reaping, Katniss is deliberately sacrificing her life to save the helpless.

After she shoots, Katniss tries to commit suicide, but Peeta, the guide who represents the hopeful, sweet voice within her, won't let her do it. "Katniss never gets to sacrifice herself. She doesn't get the heroic death. She survives – and that leaves her doing the hardest thing in the world: living in it once so many of the ones that she loves are gone" (Barnes 26-27).

Having children at the end isn't settling – it's learning to love and clinging to life, building a new family in the world where she lost the old one. It's going on. By becoming a mother, Katniss fulfills the traditional heroine's quest and becomes a leader for the next generation. She will use her father's plant guide and the new book she writes as a memorial to improve the world and try for a better future.

Theseus's reputation lived on far after his story ended: As classical Athens reached its height, Theseus was depicted as a national hero in art, literature, and more. The shrine of Theseus, built around 475 BC, displayed Theseus on his heroic adventures side by side with the Athenian resistance to the Persian invaders at Marathon. As such, he became a national icon of resistance and strength, much like Katniss the Mockingjay. In his *Parallel Lives*, meant to flatter political figures of his time, Plutarch compared Theseus to other great heroes. He noted that Theseus

> offered himself for inglorious and dishonourable servitude among insolent and cruel men when he volunteered to sail away with maidens and young boys, words cannot depict such courage, magnanimity, righteous zeal for the common good, or yearning for glory and virtue. ("Comparison of Theseus and Romulus" 1.4)

This is also Katniss's heroism.

Is Katniss a feminist icon? Certainly. In a world of Harry Potters, Percy Jacksons, Batmans and Avengers, she's a powerful girl hero. She grows and changes as her actions have consequences: in fact, dealing with the trauma makes her stronger and more relatable. The only danger is in telling her audience that being the warrior woman is the only path to power or that only fighters are worthy of respect. Saying that Katniss, as a warrior, can't marry and have children at the end is as dangerous as saying women *must* do so.

> Second-wave feminists (to generalize wildly) tended to be down on the feminine; they saw frills and pink and bows and childishness (or even, in the case of radicals like Shulamith Firestone, pregnancy itself) as part of the patriarchy's effort to infantilize and denigrate women. Third-wave feminists, on the other hand, have been (in general) more interested in reclaiming the feminine. (Berlatsky)

Third-wave feminism, letting women save the day in pink miniskirts or minivans full of kids if they wish, has led to the "girl power" stories of the nineties and beyond. Xena wears armor but is happy to bear a child, whom she defends with her life. More importantly, she fights beside sympathetic, sweet Gabrielle, a woman as strong as she is, who's on a more pacifist path. Buffy is a warrior on her series, but her friend Willow is a gifted witch and computer genius, Anya is a sultry vengeance demon, and Tara has intuitive magic and creativity, even as she cooks funny-shaped pancakes. These are all paths to power, often without a sword or bow.

In fact, *The Wizard of Oz, Narnia, Coraline, Abarat, A Great and Terrible Beauty, Wicked Lovely, The Mortal Instruments,* and other heroine's journey novels feature powerful girls who aren't trying to be warriors or tomboys. Hermione, Ginny, and Luna in *Harry Potter* are brainy witches, Violet from *A Series of Unfortunate Events* and Agatha from *Girl Genius* are inventors. Pippi Longstocking goes on marvelous, parent-free adventures, while Sookie

Stackhouse, like Nancy Drew, solves mysteries.

The heroine's journey is about defeating evil, about sacrificing one's life to protect the innocent and growing up. The path to adulthood for men and women is dangerous, magical, terrifying. It challenges questers to surrender all they are. Whether for a boy or girl, a warrior or an intellectual, this is the path of true heroism.

KATNISS ONSCREEN

The Hunger Games thundered to the third-best debut in history, making $155 million on its opening weekend. The only films to beat it were *Harry Potter and the Deathly Hallows, Part 2* ($169.1 million) and *The Dark Knight* ($158 million) (Young). Both were sequels in endlessly-long franchises, and perhaps most importantly, both featured male leads. Unlike these films, today's media excitement is over a liberated, butt-kicking girl. Hermione the sidekick and Bella the clinger have nothing on Katniss. And this film's immediate success is sending the world a message – that nonwhite main characters and a steady, self-sufficient heroine can rule the screen. It's not all about Harry Potter anymore.

Lionsgate spent $80 million to produce *The Hunger Games* and a relatively modest $45 million to market it. It made far more than the recent *Alice in Wonderland* or *Twilight* movies, which had been far more heavily hyped and merchandised. Admittedly, *The Hunger Games* series had tremendous built-in awareness, with more than 24 million copies in print domestically.

The franchise will continue, with *Catching Fire* arriving November 22, 2013. Lionsgate Films announced that *Mockingjay, Part 1* will be released November 21, 2014, and *Mockingjay, Part 2* will follow November 20, 2015. Like the *Harry Potter* and *Twilight* franchises, the last story will be split, likely to draw out the sales and media hype. As the series takes its place among the other franchises, fans have adored the movie from its first appearance. At the same time, some of its choices have created a great deal of controversy.

What's New

Adapting book to movie made all the emotions more present and poignant, particularly the youth and helplessness of all the tributes brutally killed at the Cornucopia – It's no wonder Haymitch calls it a bloodbath. The career tributes feel more menacing and callous in the movie, filled with inhuman glee as they joke about the murders they commit. For anyone who's encountered teen bullies, this is all too believable.

Cato, of course, has a new character arc as he repents his murders and realizes he's been the Capitol's pawn, as they all have. It's a reasonable moment, though some viewers have missed that Cato and the others aren't supposed to be the supervillains – understated President Snow is. The graphic violence of Cato's death and the grotesque mutts-as-tributes are toned down for the movie, but still sufficiently scary.

David Levithan speaks enthusiastically about producer Nina Jacobson, herself a fan, noting:

> It really is who really gets what this book is about. And this really is a book that could so easily have been made the wrong way, and you really had to be careful to find the right people who would make it in exactly the right way in that it would not become the thing that it's criticizing. ("Gamemaker")

This movie could have been filmed as a bloodbath glorifying teen violence. Audiences could have watched the reality show of the Games, cheering for our favorite like the Capitol audience and missing all the subversion. But this clearly isn't what's happening. Cato's speech, like Peeta's kindness and Katniss's grief all remind viewers that the film is criticizing the pain and death, not reveling in them.

The characters' growth through this testing ground of the Games drives the plot. Director Gary Ross notes:

> I just loved the story so much. There is a defiant, antiauthoritarian quality to it. I guess if you look at some of my stuff, Pleasantville probably in particular, there's a streak that runs through all that. And I'm so touched by the humanity of Katniss. As much as the firestorm or the final action sequences are incredibly riveting and enormous, it's the relationships in the book that are the most moving to me. (Valby)

Josh Hutcherson as Peeta breaks the audience's hearts with his transparent joy, fear, and selfless love. He sniffs Caesar Flickerman on camera, jokingly offers to hunt with Katniss's bow, and yet makes it clear that Haymitch has a real responsibility to fulfill. Though Katniss is the powerful hunter, Peeta brings the appeal to their team, making it truly clear that his love is saving them both.

With much of her dialogue cut, Jennifer Lawrence as Katniss does much with a little, showing her fear and faked love for Peeta in her shaky smiles. Her curtsy to the Gamemakers, casual "I'll still cook you" to Buttercup the cat, and lilting "may the odds be ever in your favor" are perfect. Of course, Cinna and Haymitch stand out from the Capitol citizens because they truly understand what's happening. Effie, by contrast, demonstrates a marvelous obliviousness to the fact that Peeta and Katniss have been condemned to death. Like so many series, we have the insiders versus the outsiders, those rare adults on the children's side and the many more who blindly tell them to follow the rules and accept the adults' judgment.

Switching out of Katniss's limited perspective gave the film a bit more scope with which to experiment. We now have new scenes – Haymitch's determination to charm the sponsors, Seneca Crane and President Snow planning their strategy. We even see Haymitch approach Crane to suggest the star-crossed lovers concept. The now-visible Gamemakers seem like bullies throwing obstacles at computer game characters to make them squirm: No sympathy, no heart, just cruel constructions. Since we can no longer access Katniss's thoughts, Haymitch's snarky written notes are perfect as he tells her how to survive. Katniss is naive about any rebellion or political influence she's staring in book one (and two for that matter), but in the film, we see her having a larger impact on the world as she salutes the camera and District Eleven responds with an uprising.

When designing the Capitol, Gary Ross called for "vast horizontal open space punctuated by buildings that are incredibly solid, heavy in mass" (Egan 49). The result is an urban downtown – gray and clean, hard lines and crisp, artless edges. With skylights and a pale tunnel, the train station is equally modern. "The [Capitol] buildings are pure advertisements of industry" production designer Phil Messina added (Egan 49). The avenue of the tributes has a vaguely Roman look, decorated with many stone staircases. All is washed out and lifeless behind the garish Capitol fashions. The Capitol looks appropriately opulent, luxurious, unwelcoming, and foreign, particularly when Katniss sees her room. It's a wonderful moment when she dials up the forest scene and gazes at it, bidding a silent goodbye to all she's lost.

The Cornucopia itself is oddly hideous and blocky – there a gaudy, tacky, Capitol-style cornucopia would have fit better, though the blocky building looks almost equally incongruous in the forest. Inside, it resembles an equipment shed, with plastic cases, shining weapons, and oddly, no food. It's clearly designed to be another token of unnatural progress. Gary Ross explained, "I wanted to create a large metallic sculptural element that almost seemed like a knife-edge into the natural world. We came up with this faceted, sculptural object that felt evocative of the Capitol: hard and cold" (Egan 67).

Fans were excited to see her two fiery outfits – the parade costumes have a textured, shiny coal look, and Katniss's eyes are outlined with flame colors. Her braids are complex, exotic and dark, a bit Greek. "I made a helmet out of [over ten different braids of] hair. It looks like a headpiece, almost Gladiator-like," Linda Flowers, the hair designer, explained (Laurence). With Katniss's pointy uniform shoulders, it looks militaryesque or armorlike, a toughening before the arena.

The flaming interview gown was a bit of a surprise for those who'd memorized the books, and it came out as a lovely effect. Of course, CGI effects and modern styling replaced the awestruck fascination Katniss has for the near-magical stitchery Cinna produces in the books. It's special effects, not craft. As one of *Slate Magazine*'s contributors notes:

> What's most disappointing about Katniss's interview dress is how it shortchanges the costume designer's art. Sure, we live in an era when you can pop computerized flames into any scene (and onto any outfit). But what a shame to rely on computer effects when there are so many luminous textiles and trims to play with: silks and sequins, chiffons and gemstones, beads and pleats and gathers. If the Hunger Games' costume designers had used the magic of fashion to create Katniss's supernaturally lovely look, the result would have been even more breathtaking – and made it that much more fun to root for her. (Turner)

The less said about the Capitol's awful yellow interview tutu, as Katniss dresses in the ridiculous fashions to show her conformity – the better.

In the film, the Avoxes wear red with a triangular slit in front and pale makeup. The red suggests pain or martyrdom, influenced by the Capitol's garish costuming. Like Katniss in her red gown, they are controlled by the Capitol rather than choosing the fashion for themselves. The slit makes them seem wounded or exploited, stabbed in the chest and walking about with the wound exposed. A red collar like a slit throat only adds to the effect.

Capitol fashions have lots of insanely bright colors with matching hair and heavy makeup – stressing their lack of grounding in reality, the citizens resemble fantastical fairies decorated in overdone flower colors. They are alien, childlike, barely attached to the world. "I was using anywhere between 400 and 450 wigs and hair extensions on set. Almost everybody had something!" the hair designer reported (Laurence). Every outfit is startling, even garish.

Cinna by contrast wears somber black, with just a little gold eyeliner, like his book character. Donald Sutherland wears an old-fashioned suit, stark and simple among the Capitol's flash. This makes him appear above all the fashion trends and austere but also pragmatic – he's a wily politician from our day and one we can understand. Likewise, Seneca Crane's militaristic uniform links him with our time with a hint of violence, rather than dressing him in Collins's science fiction robes. His fascinating Mephistopheles beard makes him appear the devil on Snow's shoulder, hastily sacrificed as Snow's scapegoat. Snow, of course, has no angel guiding him. If there is an angel, it's Rue, sacrificed in the Games.

Katniss's District Twelve, with vaguely 1940's clothes, seems to harken back to World War II and its concentration camps as the children are lined up to be sacrificed. The filmmakers show the poverty and starvation clearly, with piles of picked-over bones and faces filled with despair. The Capitol, by contrast, is science fictional and futuristic, especially the Gamemakers' lab. There, blank white space alternates with digital enhancements and interactive holograms, reminding viewers we've entered the future.

At the same time, the modern slang (probably meant to make the teen characters sympathetic and relatable) feels a bit odd. Katniss and Peeta use words like "yeah," "crush," and "okay" in a somewhat hard-to-swallow manner. It's an effective blend of history and future, though not without a few snags.

What's Missing

At the same time as the tale of Seneca Crane expands, Katniss's simplifies. In the cave, her growing love and sympathy may be true; it's hard to tell. She's hesitant but physically affectionate as she and Peeta cuddle each night. Her determination to save him at risk of herself is genuine, but also indistinguishable from the love she shows. Katniss appears to fall for Peeta, promoting the sale of "Team Peeta" and "Team Gale" shirts and other merchandise. The less subtle viewers no longer hear the thoughts of confused, rebellious Katniss unsure why she's about to eat poison berries but see instead another romantic lead swooning over a muscle-bound stud. Further, her revelation to Peeta is gone.

> In the film we see Haymitch warning Katniss that if she wants to live another day after the games she has to pretend to love Peeta forever. In the book Katniss's big "my love for you is make believe" reveal is devastating to Peeta, because he was actually in love with her. Plus, Katniss has been seemingly fanning this unrequited love by resting her head on his shoulder and flirting with him during the final interviews. On the screen we see Katniss hold Peeta's hand and say a few nice things to him, but the actual exploitation is gone from the movie (possibly to detract the audience from hating Katniss for being so cruel). Couple that with the fact that Peeta never said the iconic line, "She has no idea, the effect she can have," in the film – and you have a pretty strongly one-sided love triangle. (Woerner)

Without her feelings textualized, viewers are less certain whether she means it. Only in the final interview, with fake smile and unlikely platitudes, does her behavior appear completely an act.

Besides this, one of the most surprising losses was the lack of any explanation of the mockingjay as a symbol of rebellion against the Capitol. Katniss's pin and the mockingjays Rue and Katniss use to signal each other go unexplained. Meanwhile, Rue and Katniss no longer have the same equal partnership – Rue saves Katniss with *her* beehive idea, and then tends her in the forest for three days before she wakes, likely praying that Katniss won't kill her. There's no mention of Katniss's pin forging a bond between them (which would have been especially nice now that Prim is the giver).

Books adapted into movies have to cut a great deal; in this case the characters. Katniss's prep team, Peeta's family, Madge and the Mayor, the Avoxes are trimmed severely, if not dispensed with entirely. Gale's appearances felt short for such a central character, though it's difficult to see how they could have put more of him in. Like Jacob on *Twilight*, he'll have a larger role in the sequels. Seneca Crane is given a generous amount of screen time, more than President Snow, who appears to operate behind the scenes. Ironically, after all of Seneca's setup, he's the only non-tribute character who won't make it to the sequel.

Leaving Katniss's first person perspective behind lets the scriptwriters tell a larger, more epic story. Ross notes, "Unlike the book, the film has the luxury of being able to cut away since it's not told strictly in the first person. Lots of the things Katniss is speculating about – the gamemakers, Capitol, manipulation – a lot of that I was able to cut away to and show" (Sluis).

Without Katniss's thoughts, the movie relies on visual images to make most of its points: As everyone watches the Games, Gale sitting in a lone boycott in the forest makes a poignant image. Action is characterized by minimal tense yet subtle music punctuated with loud gasps, screams, and snapping branches. These, combined with constantly moving jerky cameras make these moments feel more realistic, rather than perfectly staged. The handheld camera and muted sounds are especially apparent during Katniss's stressful moments boarding the train, starting her interview, entering the Games. When Katniss hallucinates or is injured in the explosion, the world turns muddled and confused, drawing us in. Music remains understated throughout, like the luminous music for Rue's flower scene. David Levithan admires Gary Ross's compensation for the first person story, adding, "Between him and Jennifer Lawrence's performance, you get exactly what's in the book, so far as the experience of it through her eyes" ("Casting: The World is Watching").

A survival story makes a great book, but often a lousy movie, so most of the survival and starvation are shortened: Katniss doesn't struggle with dehydration all alone in the forest because that would film tediously. She only gets one night partnered with Rue and two with Peeta, speeding up the drama and cutting much of their struggle to find food. Any hunger or lack of supplies is only mentioned twice. In fact, despite their trainer's warning, none of the children are killed by the elements except for Foxface (technically, anyway) – almost all are murdered by the savage Careers.

In fact, food has basically vanished from the story. All right, people eating, sleeping, and using the bathroom can fit into books as summary, but has more trouble getting fleshed out into movie scenes. However, we lost some particularly poignant moments:

> It was surprising that not a single food item was namechecked in the movie. There was no reaping fish soup, no goat cheese Prim saves for her sister, no Mellark cookies, no crescent bread delivered from District 11 which was supposedly meant for little Rue (a completely gutting moment), and of course, no lamb stew! (Woerner)

There's also a bit of a plot hole when Katniss doesn't use Haymitch's magical healing ointment on Peeta – it appears to be identical to the second one she risks her life for at the Cornucopia (whereas in the book, they are quite different in form and function).

In the book, Peeta loses his leg mostly because battles have consequences – the kids can't leave wholly unscarred. The movie minimizes the trauma they both have to fight through – the teens don't starve, their wounds heal instantly from Katniss's ear to Peeta's leg, Katniss is barely aware there will be consequences for her defiance at movie's end. As such, they don't seem to have learned as much of a lesson.

In the books, Katniss horribly scarred. The face of the boy she kills haunts her and she clings to Peeta in horror as Cato's screams echo all night. Her shooting him is a more than a mercy killing – she is aghast at his pain until it takes her over: Cato is not her enemy, he is only a suffering human being "I don't care who he is or what he's done, all I want is for his suffering to end," she adds (*HG* 339). At the same time, she knows that audiences are riveted, so much so that the Gamemakers will never cut Cato's agony short. In this moment, the Games become like *The Simpsons'* Itchy and Scratchy – repellently disgusting rather than funny, and thus a commentary on the horrific things people watch as entertainment. Granted, trimming the violence was the only right way to make this a movie teens and kids could watch, but, as often happens with movies, some of the complexity has been lost.

Katniss is shown only killing in self-defense, but the repercussions are absent: gone is Katniss's remorse for Marvel, Cato, and Glimmer. The moment with the mutts-as-tributes attacking is especially horrific because of Katniss's guilt and sorrow over their deaths. In the book, the Capitol repairs "the starving, wounded mess of a person" (*HG* 350) and erases all her physical damage. Yet Katniss is still torn up inside, jumping at shadows and tense with trauma. The moments in which she faces their families on her Victory Tour and has horrific nightmares each night will likely be cut from the second film.

The quick ending, pared down to a few lines of dialogue, feels rushed and unresolved. Katniss doesn't tell Peeta her real feelings, Snow doesn't threaten her, just looks a bit pensive. Katniss's last line, in which she plans to "try to forget" is weak compared with either trying to survive Snow's next plot or lead a revolution. It's not clear enough where the characters are heading. By racing us from Games to ending credits (after Katniss and Peeta are taken up by hovercraft, there's exactly *four minutes* of movie compared with about thirty pages) viewers don't have time to digest what happened and what it means on a deep level. This is supposed to be a story about the damage caused by war, to young soldiers and desensitized viewers as well as the casualties themselves. The movie mops up too much of this loss.

Casting Issues

Even in the midst of all the media hype, there was some disturbing controversy surrounding the show. Rue and Thresh in the book are described as having "dark skin," and Collins left no doubt in interviews, saying simply, "They're African-American" (Valby). Nonetheless, many fans filled the web with comments of how they were "surprised" Rue and other characters were Black. After casting was announced, Bim Adewunmi noted in *The Guardian:*

> Many of us will have seen the racist tweets of The Hunger Games fandom over the last few days. At the risk of sounding like the veteran with the thousand-yard stare, I wasn't surprised...I am a woman of colour with a deep – almost unhealthy – love of popular culture. It is a love that is sorely tested in the face of such prejudice when I am told, loudly and with few qualms, that the stories of people who look like me just aren't viable in a specific universe. It is often explicitly stated by my co-fans that I am not – ever – what they picture when they read these books or hear about these movies. The language may be coded: "She's not how I imagined" or, in the case of interracial couple Sam and Mercedes on TV's *Glee*, slightly more explicit: "They don't look right together, like, they don't ... fit." But the message is clear. We get to be supporting characters – the redshirts – or the villains. But heroes? Um, no. That would make things too...ethnic.

Some fans were far more blatantly racist – on the film's opening weekend, Dodai Stewart noted unsettling and offensive Twitter posts such as "why does rue have to be black not gonna lie kinda ruined the movie" and "call me racist but when I found out rue was black her death wasn't as sad." Stewart adds:

> Here's what scares me...
>
> All these... people... read the Hunger Games. Clearly, they all fell in love with and cared about Rue. Though what they really fell in love with was an image of Rue that they'd created in their minds. A girl that they knew they could love and adore and mourn at the thought of knowing that she's been brutally killed.
>
> [...]
>
> These people are MAD that the girl that they cried over while reading

> the book was "some black girl" all along. So now they're angry. Wasted tears, wasted emotions. It's sad to think that had they known that she was black all along, there would have been no sorrow or sadness over her death.
>
> There are MAJOR TIE-INS to these reactions and the injustices that we see around the world today.

Beside *Harry Potter*- and *Lord of the Rings*-style white fantasy, in which the major characters don't break the race barrier (not to mention the made-up pasty skin of *Twilight* vampires), we finally get a racially diverse post-nineties style fantasy movie that depicts future America as being mixed – villains and heroes can be any race. Thresh, Rue, and Cinna, all important characters though there's only three of them, are blended into the otherwise white mix. And people post racist comments because they're disturbed by this. As for me, I remember reading that book Katniss has "straight black hair" and "olive skin." So I was "surprised" Katniss was white. As Deb Jannerson comments in "*The Hunger Games* Film Whitens its Warrior":

> In the books, Katniss is clearly not white...Katniss's ethnic background is never spelled out in familiar terms in the story, which makes sense, given that it takes place in either an alternate universe or a distant-future Earth in which former countries' names have become obsolete. Still, she is indicated to be of mixed ancestry, and her dark, olive-colored skin is mentioned repeatedly. In fact, she describes not resembling her mother and sister, who have pale skin and hair and thus could pass for members of a higher class. If this sounds like commentary on the way society treats people of color, it is, as much as the war-ravaged Panem run by the despotic "Capitol" speaks to modern politics. With Lawrence stepping into Katniss's boots, though, Collins's address of racial dynamics is likely to be lost. (Jannerson)

In fact, casting director Debra Zane posted the call for potential Katnisses as follows: "Caucasian, between ages 15 and 20," "underfed but strong," and "naturally pretty underneath her tomboyishness" (Nededog). Upon reading the description of book Katniss, Hollywood instantly decided on "Caucasian" and "underfed." Ross commented: "Thresh and Rue will be African-American. It's a multi-racial culture and the film will reflect that. But I think Suzanne didn't see a particular ethnicity to Gale and Katniss when she wrote it, and that's something we've talked about a lot" (Valby). "No particular ethnicity?" Since Katniss doesn't resemble her own mother and sister, mixed is likely (if ethnicity is even a concept in the heavily-districted future). But how does that become a Caucasian-only casting call?

Though naturally blonde and thus a far cry from racially mixed Katniss,

Jennifer Lawrence tackled the deep issues in the movie well. And, in fact, Collins was the one to cast her, after watching dozens of stars audition (Mascia).

Lawrence is also proving a strong role model for young women – despite the call for "underfed" actresses, Lawrence has no intention of perpetuating Hollywood stereotypes. Following the movie, Jennifer Lawrence gained some weight, leading to negative comments before *Catching Fire* was filmed. "A few years ago Ms. Lawrence might have looked hungry enough to play Katniss, but now, at 21, her seductive, womanly figure makes a bad fit for a dystopian fantasy about a people starved into submission," Manohla Dargis wrote in *The New York Times* (Busis).

"In Hollywood, I'm obese," Lawrence admitted. "I'm considered a fat actress" (Busis). However, Lawrence took a stand for herself. "I'm never going to starve myself for a part. I don't want little girls to be like, 'Oh, I want to look like Katniss, so I'm going to skip dinner' … I was trying to get my body to look fit and strong – not thin and underfed" (Busis). She realizes she's a role model and makes ethical choices for others as well as herself.

Lawrence was excellent, no question. But she became one of an almost-entirely white main cast, leading to problematic messages. Once again, this marks a missed opportunity for Hollywood to do some outreach and embrace tolerance. As Jannerson goes on:

> Whitewashing is not a new phenomenon in the realms of YA or film and tends to spring from a misguided notion that people of color aren't relatable to (presumably white) kids. Newsflash, Hollywood: millions love Katniss. Hopefully, Hunger Games fans who flock to the cinema won't reconceptualize her as a white warrior, just as the introduction of Diego failed to discourage all gender-policed little boys from identifying with *Dora the Explorer.* Either way, a white Katniss is a missed opportunity.

The "multi-racial culture" of current America and Collins's Panem is only somewhat reflected – Capitol citizens appear to be almost entirely white (sometimes dead white), as do tributes and the citizens of District Twelve. Collins's world of the books appears more mixed with a clearer message for readers. In fact, Katniss's District Twelve is divided in a direct racial metaphor: the "merchant class" like Peeta or Mrs. Everdeen has "light hair and blue eyes" and the working class from the Seam like Gale has "olive skin" – the lighter skinned people are wealthier, in a telling commentary on the world today. In many societies, the light-skinned people are the upper class and the darker skinned people do manual labor including mining. A woman who left the upper class to wed someone from the lower would be stigmatized, her children treated as lower class. One of these mixed-class daughters, doomed to look like her father's race, would be poised to lead the revolution.

The majority of people living under dictatorships today are people of color living in the Southern hemisphere. From those countries come the children working in sweatshops or drafted as child soldiers. Like the United States, the Capitol exploits these underprivileged children from a distance, ignoring poverty and human rights violations just so they can get their shipments of shrimp and fancy textiles.

The metaphor is continued with the Capitol's fear of insurrection, again drawn across racial lines. Caucasian teens in Districts One and Two are permitted weapons training, but even having a hunting bow in District Twelve means execution for "inciting a rebellion" (*HG* 5) District Eleven with its dark-skinned crop pickers is even more oppressive, with a thirty-five foot barbed wire fence surrounded by manned watchtowers. Its citizens live in "shacks" with warm weather, agriculture, straw hats, and orchards (*CF* 55). With Rue and Thresh's dark skin, it's difficult not to connect this place with plantations and slavery. The white Peacekeepers in their stark white uniforms guard this place carefully, knowing that the most abused people have the greatest cause to rebel.

Katniss could represent any powerless teen from Iraq to Thailand, inspired by war coverage during the time of writing. But if she's white, the metaphor of an oppressed young woman of color standing up to spoiled America's greed or defying dictatorships in her homeland vanishes.

Glimmer from the privileged districts is supposed to be blonde, dressed in luxurious gold and silver. Because of her upbringing and connections as a Career Tribute, she gets the silver bow Katniss wanted for herself. Meanwhile, Katniss, with her lower-privileged coloring, is starved and oppressed by the wealthy Capitol. It in turn is ruled by pale, *white*-haired President *Snow.* Rue and Thresh are likewise exploited and abused, though it's not clear in the book whether the majority of their district is Black or just not as bleached as the Capitol. However, the film shows an entire district of mostly Black people and eleven districts (based on their tributes) of white people. No other races exist in the movie's world. As such, it's no longer third world versus first world – it's the story of Katniss the American. She may be rebelling against the president, but the racial struggle lasts only for the few seconds of the District Eleven uprising.

MetaNarrative

"It's a TV show!" Haymitch snarls. Of course, the Games are at their base a show, meant to be watched on a screen by viewers. Gary Ross notes, "Anytime you write or direct anything, you are also the audience or the reader. You want to give them the same thrill you had when you first read the book" ("The Hunger Games Director"). We see the districts watching the Capitol's propaganda film and especially the Games. As they watch, we are reminded that we too are watching a screen. Gary Ross plays up that angle, showing Katniss's interview reflected on multiple televisions and kids playing with toy swords they bought from the merchandising department. As Katniss watches Peeta's interview onscreen she is judging his story of star-crossed lovers and reacting, much like the audience. And much like us.

Jennifer Lawrence describes how those interviews remind her of attending the 2011 Oscars: "I have hair and makeup people coming to my house every day and putting me in new, uncomfortable, weird dresses and expensive shoes, and I just shut down and raise my arms up for them to get the dress on, and pout my lips when they need to put the lipstick on," she said in *Entertainment Weekly* ("Let the Games Begin") Having Katniss played by an actress highlights her role as media icon, especially with her book two tour. As fans read about her on the web or in magazines, they are mimicking the lives of Capitol citizens gossiping about her romance or choosing her wedding dress by popular vote.

Even the lifestyle of an actor has parallels. Josh Hutcherson comments:

> Peeta has this certain belief that you can't let the circumstances you're in change what you believe in or who you are as a person, and that's my number one moral. Growing up in this business, there's a lot of times where you can have different situations and people try to change who you are. Knowing who you are is what keeps you sane and so for me it's one of my core beliefs. (Mordsley, "Hunger Games Interview 1")

Jennifer Lawrence adds, "In Hollywood it's quite weird for someone to be so open and themselves, because there's so much superficiality and 'let's pretend'" (Mordsley, "Hunger Games Interview 4"). Like her, Katniss is forced to watch every word because she knows she's always being recorded.

The training was also real, to get all the tributes ready for the role of their lives: Jennifer Lawrence learned sprinting and tree climbing, along with archery from an Olympic medalist. Ross adds: "All the tributes went through a lot of rigorous training done by a company called 87/11 and Chad Stahelski, who is a brilliant stunt coordinator. They had about six weeks of training and prep work which was really rigorous and wonderful" ("The Hunger Games Director").

More intriguing is Seneca Crane's expanded role in the first movie. Caesar Flickerman starts the movie by interviewing him; President Snow ends the movie after ordering his death. True, the Capitol's new scenes emphasize Katniss's role as a pawn in her larger dystopian world…but they also *de*emphasize Katniss.

Crane never appears in the books – he's only mentioned in *Catching Fire* because his execution demonstrates Snow's ruthlessness. Katniss hangs a dummy of him to show that she's aware of Snow's double-dealing and cruelty, and that the other Gamemakers are just as vulnerable. There's nothing more – no memorable Mephistopheles beard, no fascinating byplay between him and Snow. Why is Crane so prominent in the film?

> Because the Gamesmakers of Hollywood – the establishment of Hollywood directors, writers, and studios – don't see themselves as the willing agents of the Capitol but the great artists who suffer under the boot of their patrons, the Capitol-ists and government. So the movie meaning shifts to Seneca, the director, and the evil of President Snow, rather than the hijacking power of screened images. ("Gamesmakers Hijack Story")

John Granger, the Hogwarts Professor, sees Seneca as a tool for Ross and his helpers to tell their own story – the story of being a storyteller. Granger explains that the movie now contains the story of movie makers

> (1) as heroes martyred to the Capitol-ists they are beholden to in order to have the money they need to make films and
> (2) as victims of an oligarchic government who punishes them for telling a story 'against the grain.' ("Gamesmakers Hijack Story")

In this version, Crane is the pure Gamemaker/filmmaker, committed to making the best Hunger Games he can. He's, pleasant and personable, an expert on technology. He's open to new ideas as Haymitch sells him on star-crossed lovers. However, the evil government won't stop looking over his shoulder and controlling his life. Gary Ross personally wrote the rose garden scenes to capture this relationship, possibly projecting his own struggle into their dialogue. As Seneca just tries to make a wonderful show, Snow criticizes him for awarding Katniss an eleven in training, and utters his infamous, "I like you. Be careful." Snow lacks Crane's romantic, storytelling soul, as he makes clear in dialogue:

> Seneca Crane: Who doesn't like an underdog?
> President Snow: I don't.

Nonetheless, in their world, only Snow possesses the Gaming technology. If Seneca Crane wants to create Games, he must do it for Snow and follow his rules. Worse yet, Snow gives him an impossible job – tell a great story but not one that's *too* great, not one that inflames the oppressed districts. Contain hope, don't let Katniss become a hero, or a martyr, or a rebel. The look on Seneca's face demonstrates how clearly impossible it is. When he fails, as anyone would, he is ordered to kill himself.

Of course, he fails to follow the Capitol's orders by creating art that's *too* powerful, *too* good. Ross notes, "One of the things Suzanne created that interests me is that entertainment is the opiate of the masses. It's used to get political control. That's so much more powerful than overt repression" (Sluis). In this world, he who controls the television is king. Thus, Ross sees the entire Capitol as a place of suppressed artists struggling to speak. "If you had the soul of an artist but you were living in this culture, who would you be? You'd become Cinna," Ross explains ("The World is Watching" #3). Apparently, you'd also be Seneca.

> Seneca Crane is inserted here as the martyred artist who did the right thing per the Revolutionaries (Haymitch and the districts) and who pays the ultimate price for his crime, namely, speaking truth to power or letting art become a threat rather than a sop to the people. (Granger, "Gamesmakers Hijack Story")

Book Seneca is not a revolutionary, merely a Capitol stooge doing his job. He's a symbol that Snow will turn on his most devoted helpers as easily as he will on the enemy. Movie Seneca, rooting for Katniss the Underdog despite himself, is in danger of becoming too sympathetic to her cause, like Plutarch soon will. He marches to his death amidst churchlike organ music, gazing at the berries with a certain impassive dread. The consequences for Katniss's defiance are swift and cruel, but visited on the choiceless victim Seneca rather than Katniss, the true culprit.

Donald Sutherland describes Snow as a tester of others:

> He is 76 years old, He was two years old when the Hunger Games started. And he's looking for a successor. And he tests Wes' [Seneca's] character. "You've allowed this girl. This underdog. Do you like underdogs? You've allowed her to take some kind of position of power." ...When you fail, you die. You're not really of any use. You have your chances. It's kind of the same in this business these days, you know? You have that one chance and you either succeed or fail. (Lesnick)

Of course, this description echoes the theater business and its unforgiving nature.

In the end, *The Hunger Games* movie proved to be a well-thought out, well-cast adaptation of the book, with fun costumes we saw recreated at Halloween and a host of fantasy conferences. With camera angles, Ross kept the story close to Katniss, showing her terror and revulsion rather than glorifying the deaths and waste of the Games. The filmmakers displayed awareness of the larger themes: that kids must fend for themselves in this chilling dystopia, that history will never stop repeating, that the chattering wasteful fans of the Capitol echo all those blind to poverty and despair. We had clever moments not in the book as Haymitch writes "Call that a kiss?" and Snow offers Seneca Crane chilling glimpses of his philosophy. And the emotional moments hit everyone hard. With racial diversity and one of the most independent action heroines yet, it beats *Twilight*, *Harry Potter*, and most other franchises by a lot.

LOOKING TO THE FUTURE

"Though she won't divulge details, Collins has said she's researching a new YA series. Fans, rejoice!" (Mascia). Collins has established herself as someone who writes about the big issues, both in her children's *Gregor the Overlander* and in her international Katniss phenomenon. It's certain her next series will address more of these serious themes and attempt to change the world, much as *The Hunger Games* is already doing.

As the series grows, it's fueling political action: "In February, the World Food Programme of the UN and Lionsgate, the film's distributor, co-created a video to involve "Hunger Games" fans in ending hunger. World Vision, a Christian charity, has more than 100,000 teen "Hunger" fans lined up for an April 27 fast to end hunger" (Goodale). The Harry Potter Alliance recently launched an antihunger initiative called "Hunger is Not a Game," to revise Department of Agriculture legislation.

Levithan notes, "I think books, like Harry Potter or Hunger Games I mean, do draw in people and make them realize how meaningful books can be ("Gamemaker"). In Katniss's case, this is especially true. With every fictional death, this series and *Gregor the Overlander* remind readers that civilians and innocents around the world are suffering. "Something is significantly wrong with a creature that sacrifices its children's lives to settle its differences," Katniss protests, and this is a protest readers must take to heart (*MJ* 377). With her dramatic, touching books, Collins is calling for no less than an end to war and violence forever.

> That's what it would take. People rejecting war. Not one or two but all of them. Saying it was an unacceptable way to solve their differences. By the look of things, the human race had a lot of evolving to do before that happened. Maybe it was impossible. But maybe it wasn't. (Collins, *Code of Claw* 411)

She ends both her series with a glimmer of hope, that of a next generation of bright-eyed children. They are our best plea for peace.

WORKS CITED

Primary Sources

Aeschylus. *Eumenides*. Trans. Herbert Weir Smyth. Loeb Classical Library Volumes 145 & 146. Cambridge, MA: Harvard University Press, 1926. The Theoi Classical E-Texts Library. http://www.library.theoi.com.

Apollodorus. *The Library*. Trans. Sir James George Frazer. Loeb Classical Library Volumes 121 & 122. Cambridge, MA, Harvard University Press; London, William Heinemann Ltd. 1921. The Theoi Classical E-Texts Library. http://www.library.theoi.com.

Cashore, Kristin. *Graceling*. New York: Houghton Mifflin Harcourt, 2008.

Cass, Kiera. *The Selection*. USA: HarperTeen, 2012.

Clare, Cassandra. *City of Bones*. New York: Simon & Schuster, 2009.

Collins, Suzanne. *Catching Fire*. New York: Scholastic Press, 2009.

– . *Gregor and the Curse of the Warmbloods*. New York: Scholastic Press, 2005.

–. *Gregor and the Code of Claw*. New York: Scholastic Press, 2007.

–. *Gregor and the Marks of Secret*. New York: Scholastic Press, 2006.

–. *Gregor the Overlander*. New York: Scholastic Press, 2003.

–. *The Hunger Games*. New York: Scholastic Press, 2008.

–. *Mockingjay*. New York: Scholastic Press, 2010.

Grant, Michael. *Gone*. USA: HarperTeen, 2008.

Grant, Mira. *Feed*. New York: Orbit Books, 2010.

Hobbes, Thomas. *The Leviathan*. Ed. A.R. Waller. Cambridge: Cambridge University Press, 1904.

Houck, Colleen. *Tiger's Curse*. USA: Splinter, 2011.

The Hunger Games. Dir. Gary Ross. Written by Gary Ross and Suzanne Collins and Billy Ray. Prod. Nina Jacobson, Jon Kilik. Lionsgate, 2012. DVD.

Jung, Carl. "Psychology and Religion: West and East." USA: Yale University Press, 1938.

L' Engle, Madeline. *A Wrinkle in Time*. USA: Random House, 2005.

Lewis, C.S. *Prince Caspian*. New York: HarperCollins, 1996.

Meyer, Stephenie. *Breaking Dawn*. USA: Little, Brown Books for Young Readers, 2008.

–. *Eclipse*. USA: Little, Brown Books for Young Readers, 2007.

–. *Twilight*. USA: Hatchette Book Group, 2005.

Orwell, George. *Nineteen-Eighty-Four.* USA: Knopf, 1992.
Plutarch. *Plutarch's Lives.* Trans. Bernadotte Perrin. Cambridge, MA: Harvard University Press, 1919. *The Perseus Digital Library.* Web. http://www.perseus.tufts.edu.
Pierce, Tamora. *In the Hand of the Goddess.* New York: Alfred A. Knopf, 1989.
–. *The Woman who Rides Like a Man.* New York: Alfred A. Knopf, 1989.
Roth, Veronica. *Divergent.* New York: HarperCollins, 2011.
Shakespeare, William. *The Riverside Shakespeare,* 2nd Ed. USA: Houghton Mifflin Co, 1997.
"Sigrdrifumol." *The Poetic Edda.* Trans. Henry Adams Bellows. Princeton: Princeton University Press, 1936. The Internet Sacred Text Archive. http://www.sacred-texts.com/neu/poe/poe25.htm.
Tolkien, J.R.R. *The Return of the King.* New York: Houghton Mifflin Co., 1994.

Interviews

"A Conversation with Gary Ross and Elvis Mitchell." Disc 2, DVD Extras. *The Hunger Games.*
"A Conversation with Suzanne Collins." Scholastic Web Site. http://www.scholastic.com/thehungergames/media/qanda.pdf.
Blasingame, James, and Suzanne Collins. "An Interview with Suzanne Collins." *Journal of Adolescent & Adult Literacy* 52.8 (2009): 726-727.
Busis, Hillary. "Jennifer Lawrence: 'In Hollywood, I'm Obese'." *Popwatch* 9 Nov 2012. http://popwatch.ew.com/2012/11/09/jennifer-lawrence-weight.
"Casting: The World is Watching: Making the Hunger Games." Disc 2, DVD Extras. *The Hunger Games.*
Dominus, Susan. "Suzanne Collins's War Stories for Kids." *The New York Times* 8 April 2011. MM30.
Egan, Kate. *The Hunger Games: The Official Illustrated Movie Companion.* New York: Scholastic, 2012.
"Gamemaker: Suzanne Collins and the Hunger Games Phenomenon." Disc 2, DVD Extras. *The Hunger Games.*
Hudson, Hannah Trierweiler. "Sit Down with Suzanne Collins." *Instructor* 120.2 (2010): 51-53.
"The Hunger Games Director Gary Ross Interview." *SFX* 7 March

2012. http://www.sfx.co.uk/2012/03/07/the-hunger-games-director-gary-ross-interview.

Jordan, Tina. "Suzanne Collins on the Books She Loves." *EW's Shelf Life* 12 Aug 2010.

Laurence, Emily. "Hunger Games Hair Secrets from the Set!" Interview with Linda Flowers. *Seventeen.com.* http://www.seventeen.com/beauty/tips/exclusive-interview-linda-flowers?click=main_sr.

Lesnick, Silas. "Donald Sutherland on the Sociopolitical Importance of *The Hunger Games.*" *Comingsoon.net* 14 March 2012. http://www.comingsoon.net/news/movienews.php?id=88016.

"Let the Games Begin." *People.* Special Issue. 28 Mar. 2012: 8-29.

"Letters from the Rose Garden." Disc 2, DVD Extras. *The Hunger Games.*

Margolis, Rick. "The Last Battle." *School Library Journal* 56.8 (2010): 24-27.

Mordsley, Olivia. "The Hunger Games Interviews 1: Josh Hutcherson." *SFX* 13 Mar. 2012. http://www.sfx.co.uk/2012/03/13/the-hunger-games-interviews-1-josh-hutcherson.

–. "The Hunger Games Interview 4: Jennifer Lawrence." *SFX* 16 Mar. 2012. http://www.sfx.co.uk/2012/03/16/the-hunger-games-interview-4-jennifer-lawrence.

Secondary Sources

Adewunmi, Bim. "Why Wasn't *The Hunger Games* Cast as I Imagined in my Racist Reading?!" *Guardian.co.uk* 28 March 2012. http://www.guardian.co.uk/commentisfree/2012/mar/28/hunger-games-cast-racist-imagined.

Arrow, V. *The Panem Companion.* Dallas, TX: SmartPop, 2012.

Badonsky, Jill. "The Shadow Muse – Gifts of Your Dark Side." *Creativity Portal.* 2007. Blog Post. http://www.creativity-portal.com/bc/jill.badonsky/shadow-gifts-dark-side.html

Barkmeier, Steve. "Guest Post: The Meaning of Prim's Cat & Katniss: Mockingjay Discussion 27." *Hogwarts Professor: Thoughts for Serious Readers.* September 4, 2010. Blog Post. http://www.hogwartsprofessor.com.

Barnes, Jennifer Lynn. "Team Katniss." Wilson 13-27.

Belviso, Meg. "May the Narrative Be Ever in Your Favor: Storytelling in The Hunger Games." National Women's Studies Conference, Oakland, CA, Nov 8-11, 2012. Unpublished conference proceedings.

Berlatsky, Noah. "'Twilight' vs. 'Hunger Games': Why Do So Many Grown-Ups Hate Bella?" *The Atlantic* 15 Nov 2011. http://www.theatlantic.com/entertainment/archive/2011/11/twilight-vs-hunger-games-why-do-so-many-grown-ups-hate-bella/248439.

Bethune, Brian. "Dystopia Now." *Maclean's* 125.13/14 (9 April 2012): 84-88.

Biltereyst, Daniel. "Reality TV, Troublesome Pictures and Panics: Reappraising the Public Controversy around Reality TV in Europe." Holmes and Jermyn 91-110.

Bolen, Jean Shinoda. *Goddesses in Everywoman.* New York: Quill, 2004.

Borsellino, Mary. "Your Heart is a Weapon the Size of your Fist." Wilson 29-40.

Brennan, Sarah Rees. "Why So Hungry for the Hunger Games?" Wilson 1-12.

Buttsworth, Sara. "Cinderbella: Twilight, Fairy Tales, and the Twenty-First Century American Dream." Reagin 47-69.

Campbell, Joseph with Bill Moyers. *The Power of Myth.* Ed. Betty Sue Flowers. New York: Doubleday, 1988.

Cavender, Gray. "In Search of Community on Reality TV: America's Most Wanted and Survivor." Holmes and Jermyn 154-172.

Cochran, Kate. "An Old-Fashioned Gentleman? Edward's Imaginary History." Reagin 7-25.

Dobbs, Michael Ann. "Why Hunger Games Is the New Little House on the Prairie." *IO9* 26 April 2012. http://io9.com/5905553/why-hunger-games-is-the-new-little-house-on-the-prairie.

Dunkley, Christopher. "Reality TV." *Financial Times* 10 January 2001. 24.

Elgin, Susan. "The Secret Life of Vampires." *Newsweek* 4 Aug. 2008: 63.

Estés, Clarissa Pinkola. *Women Who Run With the Wolves.* New York: Ballantine Books, 1992.

"Exclusive: Stephen King on J.K. Rowling, Stephenie Meyer." *USA Weekend* 2 Feb. 2009. http://whosnews.usaweekend.com/2009/02/exclusive-stephen-king-on-jk-rowling-stephenie-meyer.

Frankel, Valerie Estelle. *Buffy and the Heroine's Journey.* Jefferson, NC: McFarland and Co., 2012.

–. *From Girl to Goddess: The Heroine's Journey through Myth and Legend.* Jefferson, NC: McFarland and Co., 2010.

–. *Katniss the Cattail: An Unauthorized Guide to Names and Symbols in The Hunger Games.* USA: LitCrit Press, 2012.

Freeman, Philip. *Julius Caesar.* New York: Simon & Schuster, 2008.

Goodale, Gloria. "'Hunger Games' Fandom: Can it Become a Force for Good?" *Christian Science Monitor* 22 March 2012.

Granger, John. "Gamesmakers Hijack Story: Capitol Wins Hunger Games Again" *Hogwarts Professor: Thoughts for Serious Readers.* March 27, 2012. Blog Post. http://www.hogwartsprofessor.com.

–. "Mockingjay Discussion 15: The Hanging Tree." *Hogwarts Professor: Thoughts for Serious Readers.* August 25, 2010. Blog Post. http://www.hogwartsprofessor.com.

–. "Mockingjay Discussion 13: President Hillary Coin?" *Hogwarts Professor: Thoughts for Serious Readers.* August 25, 2010. Blog Post. http://www.hogwartsprofessor.com.

–. "Mockingjay Discussion 19: Shadows of Twilight." *Hogwarts Professor: Thoughts for Serious Readers.* August 27, 2010. Blog Post. http://www.hogwartsprofessor.com.

–. "Unlocking 'The Hunger Games': The Surface, Moral, Allegorical, and Sublime Meanings." *Hogwarts Professor: Thoughts for Serious Readers.* February 22, 2010. Blog Post. http://www.hogwartsprofessor.com.

Halper, Thomas and Douglas Muzzio. "Hobbes in the City: Urban Dystopias in American Movies." *The Journal of American Culture* 30:4 (2007) 379-390.

Hardy, Elizabeth Baird. "Professor Sprout Goes to District 12 and the Arena: Some 'Hunger Games' Plant and Berry Thoughts." *Hogwarts Professor: Thoughts for Serious Readers.* September 17, 2010. Blog Post. http://www.hogwartsprofessor.com.

Hollis, James. *Tracking the Gods: The Place of Myth in Modern Life.* Toronto: Inner City Books, 1995.

Holmes, Su. "'All You've Got to Worry about is the Task, Having a Cup of Tea, and Doing a Bit of Sunbathing': Approaching Celebrity in *Big Brother.*" Holmes and Jermyn 111-135.

Holmes, Su and Deborah Jermyn, eds. *Understanding Reality Television.* New York: Routledge, 2004.

Jannerson, Deb. "*The Hunger Games* Film Whitens its Warrior." *Bitch Media* 21 March 2011. http://bitchmagazine.org/post/the-hunger-games-film-whitens-its-warrior.

Leggatt, Judith and Kristin Burnett. "Biting Bella: Treaty Negotiation, Quileute History, and Why 'Team Jacob' Is Doomed to Lose."

Reagin 26-46.
Lem, Ellyn and Holly Hassel. "'Killer' Katniss and 'Lover Boy' Peeta: Suzanne Collins's Defiance of Gender-Genred Reading." Pharr and Clark 118-127.
Lewis, Kristin. "What if The Hunger Games Were Real?" *Scholastic Scope*. 60.13 (14 May 2012): 17-19.
Mascia, Kristen. "Five Things To Know About... Hunger Games Author Suzanne Collins." *People* 77.15 (2012): 56.
Miller, Laura. "The Hunger Games" vs. "Twilight." Entertainment News. *Salon.com*. 5 Sept. 2010. http://www.salon.com/2010/09/05/hunger_games_twilight.
Murphy, Sarah Outterson. "The Child Soldier and the Self in Ender's Game and *The Hunger Games*." Pharr and Clark 199-208.
Nededog, Jethro. "The Hunger Games' Casting: Could You Be Katniss?" *Zap 2 it*. 25 February 2011. http://blog.zap2it.com/pop2it/2011/02/the-hunger-games-casting-could-you-be-katniss.html.
Parenti, Michael. *The Assassination of Julius Caesar*. New York: The New Press, 2003.
Pharr, Mary F. and Leisa A. Clark, Eds. *Of Bread, Blood and The Hunger Games: Critical Essays on the Suzanne Collins Trilogy*. Jefferson, NC: McFarland and Co., 2012.
Pollitt, Katha. "The Hunger Games' Feral Feminism." *Nation* 294.17 (23 April 2012): 10.
Reagin, Nancy R., Ed. *Twilight and History*. Hoboken, NJ: John Wiley & Sons, 2010.
Rees, Elizabeth M. "Smoke and Mirrors: Reality vs. Unreality in the Hunger Games." Wilson 41-66.
Robinson, Matthew. *How to Get on Reality TV*. New York: Random House, 2005.
Rosen, David M. *Armies of the Young: Child Soldiers in War And Terrorism*. USA: Rutgers University Press, 2005.
–. *Child Soldiers*. ABC-CLIO, Apr 23, 2012
Schecter, Barnet. *The Devil's Own Work: The Civil War Draft Riots and the Fight to Reconstruct America*. Bloomsbury Publishing USA, 2007
Seltzer, Sarah. "Hunger Pangs: Hunting for the Perfect Heroine." *Bitch Magazine: Feminist Response to Pop Culture*. 51 (Summer 2011): 38-42.
Singer, P.W. *Children at War*. New York: Pantheon Books, 2005.
Sluis, Sarah. "Appetite for Dystopia: Gary Ross Creates a Ruthless

World in Eagerly Awaited Hunger Games." *Film Journal International* 115.3 (Mar 2012): 8-12. *Academic Search Premiere.* Web.

Springen, Karen. "Apocalypse Now." *Publishers Weekly* 257.7 (2010): 21-24. *Academic Search Premiere.* Web.

Stewart, Dodai. "Racist Hunger Games: Fans Are Very Disappointed." *Jezebel.com* 26 Mar. 2012. http://jezebel.com/5896408/racist-hunger-games-fans-dont-care-how-much-money-the-movie-made.

Turner, Julia. "Why Katniss's Costumes Are All Wrong." *Browbeat: Slate's Culture Blog* 27 March 2012. http://www.slate.com/blogs/browbeat/2012/03/27/katniss_costumes_in_the_hunger_games_weren_t_nearly_awesome_enough.html.

Vizzini, Ned. "Reality Hunger: Authenticity, Heroism, and Media in the Hunger Games." Wilson 81-98.

Walker, Barbara G. *The Woman's Dictionary of Symbols and Sacred Objects.* San Francisco: Harper, 1988.

Wessells, Michael G. *Child Soldiers: From Violence to Protection.* Harvard: Harvard University Press, 2006.

Wilson, Leah, Ed. *The Girl Who Was on Fire: Your Favorite Authors on Suzanne Collins's Hunger Games Trilogy.* Dallas, TX: SmartPop, 2011.

Wilson, Natalie. "Eating Up the Hunger Games, Romance and All." *Ms. Magazine Blog* 23 March 2012. http://msmagazine.com/blog/blog/2012/03/23/eating-up-the-hunger-games-romance-and-all.

Wloszczyna, Susan. "Classic Romantic Triangle Takes Monstrous Form in 'New Moon'." *USA Today* 15 Nov. 2009. http://abcnews.go.com/Entertainment/love-triangle-looms-twilights-moon/story?id=9076121#.UDPa191lRn8.

Woerner, Meredith. "Everything The Hunger Games Movie Left Out." *IO9* 26 Mar. 2012. http://io9.com/5896475/everything-the-hunger-games-movie-left-out.

Young, John. "Box Office Report: 'The Hunger Games' Posts Third-best Opening Weekend Ever with $155 Mil." *Entertainment Weekly.com* 25 Mar. 2012. http://insidemovies.ew.com/2012/03/25/box-office-report-hunger-games.

INDEX

Other Titles of Interest

C. S. Lewis: Views From Wake Forest - Essays on C. S. Lewis
Michael Travers, editor

Contains sixteen scholarly presentations from the international C. S. Lewis convention in Wake Forest, NC. Walter Hooper shares his important essay "Editing C. S. Lewis," a chronicle of publishing decisions after Lewis' death in 1963.

"Scholars from a variety of disciplines address a wide range of issues. The happy result is a fresh and expansive view of an author who well deserves this kind of thoughtful attention."
Diana Pavlac Glyer, author of *The Company They Keep*

The Hidden Story of Narnia:
A Book-By-Book Guide to Lewis' Spiritual Themes
Will Vaus

A book of insightful commentary equally suited for teens or adults – Will Vaus points out connections between the *Narnia* books and spiritual/biblical themes, as well as between ideas in the *Narnia* books and C. S. Lewis' other books. Learn what Lewis himself said about the overarching and unifying thematic structure of the Narnia books. That is what this book explores; what C. S. Lewis called "the hidden story" of Narnia. Each chapter includes questions for individual use or small group discussion.

Why I Believe in Narnia:
33 Reviews and Essays on the Life and Work of C. S. Lewis
James Como

Chapters range from reviews of critical books, documentaries and movies to evaluations of Lewis' books to biographical analysis.

"A valuable, wide-ranging collection of essays by one of the best informed and most acute commentators on Lewis' work and ideas."
Peter Schakel, author of *Imagination & the Arts in C. S. Lewis*

C. S. Lewis Goes to Heaven: A Reader's Guide to The Great Divorce
David G. Clark

This is the first book devoted solely to this often neglected book and the first to reveal several important secrets Lewis concealed within the story. Lewis felt his imaginary trip to Hell and Heaven was far better than his book *The Screwtape Letters*, which has become a classic. Clark is an ordained minister who has taught courses on Lewis for more than 30 years and is a New Testament and Greek scholar with a Doctor of Philosophy degree in Biblical Studies from the University of Notre Dame. Readers will discover the many literary and biblical influences Lewis utilized in writing his brilliant novel.

C. S. Lewis & Philosophy as a Way of Life
Adam Barkman

C. S. Lewis is rarely thought of as a "philosopher" per se despite having both studied and taught philosophy for several years at Oxford. Lewis's long journey to Christianity was essentially philosophical – passing through seven different stages. This 624 page book is an invaluable reference for C. S. Lewis scholars and fans alike

C. S. Lewis: His Literary Achievement
Colin Manlove

"This is a positively brilliant book, written with splendor, elegance, profundity and evidencing an enormous amount of learning. This is probably not a book to give a first-time reader of Lewis. But for those who are more broadly read in the Lewis corpus this book is an absolute gold mine of information. The author gives us a magnificent overview of Lewis' many writings, tracing for us thoughts and ideas which recur throughout, and at the same time telling us how each book differs from the others. I think it is not extravagant to call C. S. Lewis: His Literary Achievement a tour de force."

Robert Merchant, *St. Austin Review*, Book Review Editor

Mythopoeic Narnia:
Memory, Metaphor, and Metamorphoses in The Chronicles of Narnia
Salwa Khoddam

Dr. Khoddam, the founder of the C. S. Lewis and Inklings Society (2004), has been teaching university courses using Lewis' books for over 25 years. Her book offers a fresh approach to the Narnia books based on an inquiry into Lewis' readings and use of classical and Christian symbols. She explores the literary and intellectual contexts of these stories, the traditional myths and motifs, and places them in the company of the greatest Christian mythopoeic works of Western literature. In Lewis' imagination, memory and metaphor interact to advance his purpose – a Christian metamorphosis. *Mythopoeic Narnia* helps to open the door for readers into the magical world of the Western imagination.

Speaking of Jack: A C. S. Lewis Discussion Guide
Will Vaus

C. S. Lewis societies have been forming around the world since the first one started in New York City in 1969. Will Vaus has started and led three groups himself. *Speaking of Jack* is the result of Vaus' experience in leading those Lewis societies. Included here are introductions to most of Lewis' books as well as questions designed to stimulate discussion about Lewis' life and work. These materials have been "road-tested" with real groups made up of young and old, some very familiar with Lewis and some newcomers. *Speaking of Jack* may be used in an existing book discussion group, to start a C. S. Lewis society, or to guide your own exploration of Lewis' books.

George MacDonald

Diary of an Old Soul & The White Page Poems
George MacDonald and Betty Aberlin

The first edition of George MacDonald's book of daily poems included a blank page opposite each page of poems. Readers were invited to write their own reflections on the "white page." MacDonald wrote: "Let your white page be ground, my print be seed, growing to golden ears, that faith and hope may feed." Betty Aberlin responded to MacDonald's invitation with daily poems of her own.

"Betty Aberlin's close readings of George MacDonald's verses and her thoughtful responses to them speak clearly of her poetic gifts and spiritual intelligence."
Luci Shaw, poet

George MacDonald: Literary Heritage and Heirs
Roderick McGillis, editor

This latest collection of 14 essays sets a new standard that will influence MacDonald studies for many more years. George MacDonald experts are increasingly evaluating his entire corpus within the nineteenth century context.

"This comprehensive collection represents the best of contemporary scholarship on George MacDonald."
Rolland Hein, author of *George MacDonald: Victorian Mythmaker*

In the Near Loss of Everything: George MacDonald's Son in America
Dale Wayne Slusser

In the summer of 1887, George MacDonald's son Ronald, newly engaged to artist Louise Blandy, sailed from England to America to teach school. The next summer he returned to England to marry Louise and bring her back to America. On August 27, 1890, Louise died, leaving him with an infant daughter. Ronald once described losing a beloved spouse as "the near loss of everything." Dale Wayne Slusser unfolds this poignant story with unpublished letters and photos that give readers a glimpse into the close-knit MacDonald family.

A Novel Pulpit: Sermons From George MacDonald's Fiction
David L. Neuhouser

"In MacDonald's novels, the Christian teaching emerges out of the characters and story line, the narrator's comments, and inclusion of sermons given by the fictional preachers. The sermons in the novels are shorter than the ones in collections of MacDonald's sermons and so are perhaps more accessible for some. In any case, they are both stimulating and thought-provoking. This collection of sermons from ten novels serve to bring out the 'freshness and brilliance' of MacDonald's message."
From the author's introduction

Behind the Back of the North Wind:
Critical Essays on George MacDonald's Classic Children's Book
John Pennington and Roderick McGillis, editors

The unique blend of fairy tale atmosphere and social realism in this novel laid the groundwork for modern fantasy literature. Sixteen essays by various authors are accompanied by an instructive introduction, extensive index, and beautiful illustrations.

Through the Year with George MacDonald: 366 Daily Readings
Rolland Hein, editor

These page-length excerpts from sermons, novels and letters are given an appropriate theme/heading and a complementary Scripture passage for daily reading. An inspiring introduction to the artistic soul and Christian vision of George MacDonald.

Christian Living

The Living Word of the Living God: A Beginner's Guide to Reading and Understanding the Bible
Rev. Tom Furrer

This book is based on over 20 years experience of teaching the Bible to confirmation classes at Episcopal churches in Connecticut. Chapters from Genesis to Revelation.

Keys to Growth: Meditations on the Acts of the Apostles
Will Vaus

Every living things or person requires certain ingredients in order to grow, and if a thing or person is not growing, it is dying. *The Acts of the Apostles* is a book that is all about growth. Will Vaus has been meditating and preaching on *Acts* for the past 30 years. In this volume, he offers the reader forty-one keys from the entire book of Acts to unlock spiritual growth in everyday life.

Open Before Christmas: Devotional Thoughts For The Holiday Season
Will Vaus

Author Will Vaus seeks to deepen the reader's knowledge of Advent and Christmas leading up to Epiphany. Readers are provided with devotional thoughts for each day that help them to experience this part of the Church Year perhaps in a kore spiritually enriching way than ever before.

"Seasoned with inspiring, touching, and sometimes humorous illustrations .... I found his writing immediately engaging and, the more I read, the more I liked it. God has touched my heart by reading Open Before Christmas, and I believe he will touch your heart too."

The Rev. David Beckmann, Founder of The C.S. Lewis Society of Chattanooga

Called to Serve: Life as a Firefighter-Deacon
Deacon Anthony R. Surozenski

Called to Serve is the story of one man's dream to be a firefighter. But dreams have a way of taking detours – so Tony Surozenski became a teacher and eventually a volunteer firefighter. And when God enters the picture, Tony is faced with a choice. Will he give up firefighting to follow another call? After many years, Tony's two callings are finally united – in service as a fire chaplain at Ground Zero after the 9-11 attacks and in other ways he could not have imagined. Tony is Chief Chaplain's aid for the Massachusetts Corp of Fire Chaplains and Director for the Office of the Diaconate of the Diocese of Worchester, Massachusetts.

Harry Potter

The Order of Harry Potter: The Literary Skill of the Hogwarts Epic
Colin Manlove

Colin Manlove, a popular conference speaker and author of over a dozen books, has earned an international reputation as an expert on fantasy and children's literature. His book, *From Alice to Harry Potter*, is a survey of 400 English fantasy books. In *The Order of Harry Potter*, he compares and contrasts *Harry Potter* with works by "Inklings" writers J.R.R. Tolkien, C.S. Lewis and Charles Williams; he also examines Rowling's treatment of the topic of imagination; her skill in organization and the use of language; and the book's underlying motifs and themes.

Harry Potter & Imagination: The Way Between Two Worlds
Travis Prinzi

Imaginative literature places a reader between two worlds: the story world and the world of daily life, and challenges the reader to imagine and to act for a better world. Starting with discussion of Harry Potter's more important themes, *Harry Potter & Imagination* takes readers on a journey through the transformative power of those themes for both the individual and for culture by placing Rowling's series in its literary, historical, and cultural contexts.

Repotting Harry Potter: A Professor's Guide for the Serious Re-Reader
Rowling Revisited: Return Trips to Harry, Fantastic Beasts, Quidditch, & Beedle the Bard
James W. Thomas

In *Repotting Harry Potter* and his sequel book *Rowling Revisited*, Dr. James W. Thomas points out the humor, puns, foreshadowing and literary parallels in the Potter books. In *Rowling Revisited*, readers will especially find useful three extensive appendixes – "Fantastic Beasts and the Pages Where You'll Find Them," "Quidditch Through the Pages," and "The Books in the Potter Books." Dr. Thomas makes re-reading the Potter books even more rewarding and enjoyable.

The Deathly Hallows Lectures:
The Hogwarts Professor Explains Harry's Final Adventure
John Granger

In *The Deathly Hallows Lectures*, John Granger reveals the finale's brilliant details, themes, and meanings. *Harry Potter* fans will be surprised by and delighted with Granger's explanations of the three dimensions of meaning in *Deathly Hallows*. Ms. Rowling has said that alchemy sets the "parameters of magic" in the series; after reading the chapter-length explanation of *Deathly Hallows* as the final stage of the alchemical Great Work, the serious reader will understand how important literary alchemy is in understanding Rowling's artistry and accomplishment.

Sociology and Harry Potter: 22 Enchanting Essays on the Wizarding World
Jenn Simms, editor

Modeled on an Introduction to Sociology textbook. this books is not simply about the series, but also used the series to facilitate reader's understanding of the discipline of sociology and a development of a sociological approach to viewing social reality. It is a case of high quality academic scholarship written in a form and on a topic accessible to non-academics. As such, it is written to appeal to Harry Potter fans and the general reading public. Contributors include professional sociologists from eight countries.

Harry Potter, Still Recruiting:
An Inner Look at Harry Potter Fandom
Valerie Frankel, editor

The Harry Potter phenomenon has created a new world: one of Quidditch in the park, lightning earrings, endless parodies, a new genre of music, and fan conferences of epic proportions. This book attempts to document everything - exploring costuming, crafting, gaming, and more, with essays and interviews straight from the multitude of creators. From children to adults, fans are delighting the world with an explosion of captivating activities and experiences, all based on Rowling's delightful series.

Hog's Head Conversations: Essays on Harry Potter
Travis Prinzi, editor

Ten fascinating essays on Harry Potter are divided into five sections: Conversations on 1) Literary Value, 2) Eternal Truth, 3) Imagination, 4) Literary Criticism, and 5) Characters. Contributors include the following popular Potter writers and speakers: John Granger, James W. Thomas, Colin Manlove, and Travis Prinzi.

Biography

Sheldon Vanauken: The Man Who Received "A Severe Mercy"
Will Vaus

In this biography we discover: Vanauken the struggling student, the bon-vivant lover, the sailor who witnessed the bombing of Pearl Harbor, the seeker who returned to faith through C. S. Lewis, the beloved professor of English literature and history, the feminist and anti-war activist who participated in the March on the Pentagon, the bestselling author, and Vanauken the convert to Catholicism. What emerges is the portrait of a man relentlessly in search of beauty, love, and truth, a man who believed that, in the end, he found all three.

"This is a charming biography about a doubly charming man who wrote a triply charming book. It is a great way to meet the man behind A Severe Mercy."

Peter Kreeft, author of *Jacob's Ladder: 10 Steps to Truth*

Poets and Poetry

Remembering Roy Campbell: The Memoirs of his Daughters, Anna and Tess
Introduction by Judith Lütge Coullie, editor
Preface by Joseph Pearce

Anna and Teresa Campbell were the daughters of the handsome young South African poet and writer, Roy Campbell (1901-1957), and his beautiful English wife, Mary Garman. In their frank and moving memoirs, Anna and Tess recall the extraordinary, and often very difficult, lives they shared with their exceptional parents. The book includes over 50 photos, 344 footnotes, a timeline of Campbell's life, and a complete index.

In the Eye of the Beholder: How to See the World Like a Romantic Poet
Louis Markos

Born out of the French Revolution and its radical faith that a nation could be shaped and altered by the dreams and visions of its people, British Romantic Poetry was founded on a belief that the objects and realities of our world, whether natural or human, are not fixed in stone but can be molded and transformed by the visionary eye of the poet. Unlike many of the books written on Romanticism, which devote many pages to the poets and few pages to their poetry, the focus here is firmly on the poems themselves. The author thereby draws the reader intimately into the life of these poems. A separate bibliographical essay is provided for readers listing accessible biographies of each poet and critical studies of their work.

The Cat on the Catamaran: A Christmas Tale
John Martin

Here is a modern-day parable of a modern-day cat with modern-day attitudes. Riverboat Dan is a "cool" cat on a perpetual vacation from responsibility. He's *The Cat on the Catamaran* – sailing down the river of life. Dan keeps his guilty conscience from interfering with his fun until he runs into trouble. But will he have the courage to believe that it's never too late to change course? (For ages 10 to adult)

"This book is a joy, and as companionable as a good-natured cat."
Walter Hooper, author of *C. S. Lewis: Companion and Guide*

The Half Blood Poems
Inspired by the Stories of J.K. Rowling
Christine Lowther

Like Harry Potter, Christine's poetry can soar above the tragic to discover the heroic and beautiful in such poems as "Neville, Unlikely Rebel", "For Our Wide-Armed Mothers," and "A Boy's Hands." There are 71 poems divided into seven chapters that correspond to the seven books. Fans of Harry Potter will experience once again many of the emotions they felt reading the books – emotions presented most effectively through a poet's words.

Pop Culture

To Love Another Person: A Spiritual Journey Through Les Miserables
John Morrison

The powerful story of Jean Valjean's redemption is beloved by readers and theatergoers everywhere. In this companion and guide to Victor Hugo's masterpiece, author John Morrison unfolds the spiritual depth and breadth of this classic novel and broadway musical.

Through Common Things: Philosophical Reflections on Popular Culture
Adam Barkman

"Barkman presents us with an amazingly wide-ranging collection of philosophical reflections grounded in the everyday things of popular culture – past and present, eastern and western, factual and fictional. This is an informative and entertaining book to read!"
Doug Bloomberg, Professor of Philosophy, Institute for Christian Studies

Above All Things: Essays on Christian Ethics and Popular Culture
Adam Barkman

"Those who don't normally think of themselves as philosophically inclined will be surprised and delighted as Barkman rescues philosophy from dry classroom abstractions and reveals how it fills the glorious messiness of everyday life."
Dr. Kevin Flatt, Assistant Professor of History, Redeemer University College

Spotlight:
A Close-up Look at the Artistry and Meaning of Stephenie Meyer's Twilight Novels
John Granger

Stephenie Meyer's *Twilight* saga has taken the world by storm. But is there more to *Twilight* than a love story for teen girls crossed with a cheesy vampire-werewolf drama? *Spotlight* reveals the literary backdrop, themes, artistry, and meaning of the four Bella Swan adventures. *Spotlight* is the perfect gift for serious *Twilight* readers.

Virtuous Worlds: The Video Gamer's Guide to Spiritual Truth
John Stanifer

Shows readers specific parallels between Christian faith and the content of their favorite games. Written with wry humor, this book will appeal to gamers and non-gamers alike. Those unfamiliar with video games may be pleasantly surprised to find that many elements in those "virtual worlds" also qualify them as "virtuous worlds."

CPSIA information can be obtained at www.ICGtesting.com
Printed in the USA
BVOW05s0747301214

381315BV00004B/265/P

9 781936 294220